Common
Sense
Economics

Revised Edition

Common Sense Economics

*What Everyone Should Know
About Wealth and Prosperity*

JAMES D. GWARTNEY
FLORIDA STATE UNIVERSITY

RICHARD L. STROUP
NORTH CAROLINA STATE UNIVERSITY

DWIGHT R. LEE
SOUTHERN METHODIST UNIVERSITY

TAWNI H. FERRARINI
NORTHERN MICHIGAN UNIVERSITY

ST. MARTIN'S PRESS NEW YORK

COMMON SENSE ECONOMICS. Copyright © 2005 and 2010 by James D. Gwartney, Richard L. Stroup, Dwight R. Lee, and Tawni H. Ferrarini. All rights reserved. Printed in the United States of America. For information, address St. Martin's Press, 175 Fifth Avenue, New York, N.Y. 10010.

www.stmartins.com

Library of Congress Cataloging-in-Publication Data

Common sense economics : what everyone should know about wealth and prosperity / James D. Gwartney . . . [et al.].—Rev. ed.
      p. cm.
   Prev. ed. entered under James D. Gwartney.
   Includes bibliographical references and index.
   ISBN 978-0-312-64489-5
   1. Free enterprise.   2. Wealth.   3. Economics.   4. Finance, Personal.
5. Saving and investment.   I. Gwartney, James D.   II. Gwartney, James D.
Common sense economics.
   HB95.G9   2010
   330—dc22

                                                        2010021851

First Edition: August 2010

10   9   8   7   6   5   4   3   2

*Dedicated to our students, past,
present, and future*

Contents

Preface

Why Should You Read This Book?

We know that your time is valuable. Most of you do not want to spend a lot of time learning new terms, memorizing formulas, or mastering details that are important only to professional economists. What you want are the insights of economics that really matter—those that will help you make better personal choices and improve your understanding of our complex world. And you want those insights to be presented in a concise, organized, and readable manner, with a minimum of economics jargon. We wrote this book to meet these objectives.

You can profit from this book regardless of your current knowledge of economics. This book will introduce a beginner to the basic principles of economics, principles that mainly reflect common sense. But these concepts are powerful tools for logical thinking that will quickly make it possible for even beginners to distinguish between sound economics and romantic nonsense. This book will also help more advanced students of economics and business pull together the big picture. Advanced students, including some at the graduate level, are often so busy with graphs, formulas, models, and technical mathematics that they fail to understand the really important lessons of economics. Finally, an experienced business executive or a policy maker can also learn much of value from this book. Even those who are highly successful at their jobs often underestimate the far-reaching, typically unintended effects that political rules and policies have on the broader economic health of people and nations.

Now, as in the past, two visions are competing for the minds and hearts of Americans. One is of limited government, economic freedom, and personal responsibility; the other, expanding government, collectivism, and dependency. America was founded on the first, but the second has been in ascendance for at least a century. Under the first vision, the economy will be directed by personal choices coordinated by markets; under the second, by central planning and politics. It makes a big difference. As the renowned Stanford economist Thomas Sowell has put it, "The first law of economics is scarcity, and the first law of politics is to disregard the first law of economics."

We have better knowledge about how these two alternatives work than at any time in history. But we are a nation of economic illiterates. As a result, we are easily misled by leaders who tell us of their good intentions—their passion to solve our problems. One of the twentieth century's greatest economists, Milton Friedman, once stated, "There's nothing that does so much harm as good intentions." This was his way of stressing that policies should be evaluated on the basis of their effectiveness, not the intentions of their proponents.

President Herbert Hoover, Senator Reed Smoot, and Congressman Willis Hawley had good intentions when they pushed the Smoot-Hawley tariff increases through Congress in 1930. Nonetheless, the consequences of this legislation were disastrous; it helped turn what should have been a normal downturn into a decade of pain and suffering. The eighteenth-century surgeons also had good intentions; they thought amputations with instruments bathed in wine would prevent diseases from getting into the blood of their patients. But their good intentions did not protect their patients from the adverse affects of their treatments. Neither will the good intentions of modern-day politicians protect us from the consequences of harmful policies.

The massive government intervention leading up to, and following, the economic crisis of 2008 has generated an increasingly urgent need for basic economic education. Our democracy puts voters in charge of choosing our policy makers, so the consequences of economic illiteracy can be disastrous. People who do not understand the sources of economic prosperity are susceptible to schemes that undermine both their own prosperity and that of their country. A nation of economic illiterates is unlikely to remain prosperous for very long.

If you are concerned about the direction of America and would like to see a road map for a more economically free and prosperous future, this book provides it. The basic principles explained here will help you better understand what types of economic arrangements work, what restraints on the political process are needed to strengthen and preserve them, and thus why some nations prosper while others stagnate or even regress. As a result, you will be able to make wiser choices as a citizen. But basic economics will also help you make better choices with regard to your consumption, saving, investments, career alternatives, and many other dimensions of personal decision making. As we explain in Part IV, economics provides some simple rules on how to build and grow wealth. And in a market economy, increasing your wealth helps others become wealthy too.

There is a website, http://CommonSenseEconomics.com, that accompanies this book. For those who want to dig deeper, the site includes supplementary units that address specific subjects such as gross domestic product, measurement of inflation, banking and monetary policy, the Great Depression, and the Economic Crisis of 2008. (Note: the full list of these topics is given in the back of this book.) These supplementary units were developed at the request of instructors using *Common Sense Economics* as a text who wanted a more comprehensive analysis of various topics. This material will meet this demand and provide instructors with maximum flexibility for the development of their course. The CSE website also includes numerous other features such as study questions, a secured instructor's test bank, links to videos, classic readings that can be downloaded to MP3 players, and many other features that will make economics livelier for both students and instructors. Our goal is to make economics fun, as well as enlightening.

—James D. Gwartney, Richard L. Stroup,
Dwight R. Lee, and Tawni H. Ferrarini
April 2010

PART I

*Twelve Key Elements
of Economics*

TWELVE KEY ELEMENTS OF ECONOMICS

1. Incentives matter.

2. There is no such thing as a free lunch.

3. Decisions are made at the margin.

4. Trade promotes economic progress.

5. Transaction costs are an obstacle to trade.

6. Prices bring the choices of buyers and sellers into balance.

7. Profits direct businesses toward activities that increase wealth.

8. People earn income by helping others.

9. Production of goods and services people value, not just jobs, provides the source of high living standards.

10. Economic progress comes primarily through trade, investment, better ways of doing things, and sound economic institutions.

11. The "invisible hand" of market prices directs buyers and sellers toward activities that promote the general welfare.

12. Too often the long-term consequences, or the secondary effects, of an action are ignored.

Introduction

Life is about choices, and economics is about how incentives affect those choices and shape our lives. Choices about education, how we spend and invest, what we do in the workplace, and many other personal decisions will influence our well-being and quality of life. Moreover, the choices we make as voters and citizens affect the laws or "rules of the game," and these rules exert an enormous impact on our freedom and prosperity. To choose intelligently, both for ourselves and for society generally, we must understand some basic principles about how people choose, what motivates their actions, and how their actions influence their personal welfare and that of others. Thus, economics is about human decision making, the analysis of the forces underlying choice, and the implications with regard to how societies work.

The following section introduces twelve key concepts that are crucial to the understanding of how our economy works. The reader will learn such things as the true meaning of costs, why prices matter, how trade furthers prosperity, and why production of things people value underpins our standard of living. In a fraction of the time devoted to Economics 101, you can pick up most of its important lessons. In subsequent sections you will use these concepts to address other vitally important topics.

1. Incentives Matter.

All of economics rests on one simple principle: Changes in incentives influence human behavior in predictable ways. Both monetary and non-monetary factors influence incentives. If something becomes more costly, people will be less likely to choose it. Correspondingly, when an option becomes more attractive, people will be more likely to choose it. This simple idea, sometimes called the basic postulate of economics, is a powerful tool because it applies to almost everything that we do.

People will be less likely to choose an option as it becomes more costly. Think about the implications of this proposition. When late for an appointment, a person will be less likely to take time to stop and visit with a friend. Fewer people will go picnicking on a cold and rainy day. Higher prices will reduce the number of units sold. Attendance in college classes will be below normal the day before spring break. In each case, the explanation is the same: As the option becomes more costly, less is chosen.

Similarly, when the payoff derived from a choice increases, people will be more likely to choose it. A person will be more likely to bend over and pick up a quarter than a penny. Students will attend and pay more attention in class when the material is covered extensively on exams. Customers will buy more from stores that offer low prices, high quality service, and a convenient location. Employees will work harder and more efficiently when they are rewarded for doing so. All of these outcomes are highly predictable and they merely reflect the "incentives matter" postulate of economics.

This basic postulate explains how changes in market prices alter incentives in a manner that works to coordinate the actions of buyers and sellers. If buyers want to purchase more of an item than producers are willing (or able) to sell, its price will soon rise. As the price increases, sellers will be more willing to provide the item while buyers purchase fewer, until the higher price brings the amount demanded and the amount supplied into balance. At that point the price stabilizes.

What happens if it starts out the other way? If an item's price is too high, suppliers will have to lower the price in order to sell it. The lower price will encourage people to buy more—but it will also discourage producers from producing as much, since at the new, lower price it will be less profitable to supply the product. Again, the price change works to bring the amount demanded by consumers into balance with the amount produced by suppliers. At that point there is no further pressure for a price change.

Remember the record high nominal gas prices in the summer of 2008? While a lot of people felt the pain of higher prices at the pump, there was no panic in the streets or lines at the gas pumps. Why? When the higher prices made it more costly to purchase gasoline, most consumers eliminated some less important trips. Others arranged more carpooling. With time, consumers also shifted to smaller, more fuel-efficient cars in order to reduce their gasoline bills. As buyers reacted to higher gas prices, so did sellers. The oil companies supplying gasoline increased their drilling, adopted new techniques to recover more oil from existing wells, and intensified their search for new oil fields. The higher price helped to keep the quantity supplied in line with the quantity demanded. Eventually, the prices of both crude oil and gasoline fell as supply expanded over time.

Incentives also influence political choices. There is little reason to believe that a person making choices in the voting booth will behave much differently than when making choices in the shopping mall. In most cases voters are more likely to support political candidates and policies that they believe will provide them with the most personal benefits, net of their costs. They will tend to oppose political options when the personal costs are high compared to the benefits they expect to receive. For example, polls indicated that nonunion members were overwhelmingly opposed to exempting union members from health care taxes that nonmembers and others were required to pay. Similarly, senior citizens have voted numerous times against candidates and proposals that would reduce their Medicare benefits.

There's no way to get around the importance of incentives. It's a part of human nature. Interestingly, incentives matter just as much under socialism as under capitalism. In the former Soviet Union, managers and employees of glass plants were at one time rewarded according to the tons of sheet glass they produced. Because their revenues depended on the weight of the glass, most factories produced sheet glass so thick that you could hardly see through it. The rules were changed so that the managers were compensated according to the number of square meters of glass they could produce. Under these rules, Soviet firms made glass so thin that it broke easily.

Some people think that incentives matter only when people are greedy and selfish. That's not true. People act for a variety of reasons, some selfish and some charitable. The choices of both the self-centered and altruistic will be influenced by changes in personal costs and benefits. For example, both the selfish and the altruistic will be more likely to attempt to rescue a child in a shallow swimming pool than in the rapid currents approaching Niagara Falls. And both are more likely to give a needy person their hand-me-downs rather than their best clothes.

Even though no one would have accused the late Mother Teresa of greediness, her self-interest caused her to respond to incentives, too. When Mother Teresa's organization, the Missionaries of Charity, attempted to open a shelter for the homeless in New York City, the city required expensive (but unneeded) alterations to its building. The organization abandoned the project. This decision did not reflect any change in Mother Teresa's commitment to the poor. Instead, it reflected a change in incentives. When the cost of helping the poor in New York went up, Mother Teresa decided that her resources would do more good in other uses.[1] Changes in incentives influence everyone's choices, regardless of the mix of greedy materialistic goals on the one hand and compassionate, altruistic goals on the other, that drive a specific decision.

2. There Is No Such Thing as a Free Lunch.

The reality of life on our planet is that productive resources are limited, while the human desire for goods and services is virtually unlimited. Would you like to have some new clothes, a luxury boat, or a vacation in the Swiss Alps? How about more time for leisure, recreation, and travel? Do you dream of driving your brand-new Porsche into the driveway of your oceanfront house? Most of us would like to have all of these things and many others! However, we are constrained by the scarcity of resources, including a limited availability of time.

Because we cannot have as much of everything as we would like, we are forced to choose among alternatives. There is no free lunch. Doing one thing makes us sacrifice the opportunity to do something else we value. This is why economists refer to all costs as opportunity costs.

Many costs are measured in terms of money, but these too are opportunity costs. The money you spend on one purchase is money that is not available to spend on other things. The opportunity cost of your purchase is the value you place on the items that must now be given up because you spent the money on the initial purchase. But just because you don't have to spend money to do something does not mean the action is costless. You don't have to spend money to take a walk and enjoy a beautiful sunset, but there is an opportunity cost to the walk. The time you spend walking could have been used to do something else you value, like visiting a sick friend or reading a book.

We often hear it said that some things are so important that we should do them without considering the cost. Making such a statement may sound reasonable at first thought, and may be an effective way to encourage government to spend more money on things that you value and would like others to help pay for. But the unreasonableness of ignoring cost becomes obvious once we recognize that costs are the value of forgone alternatives. Saying that we do something without considering the cost just says that we should do it without considering the alternatives.

The choices of both consumers and producers involve costs. For consumers, the cost of a good, as reflected in its price, helps us compare our desire for a product against our desire for alternative products that we could purchase instead. If we do not consider the costs, we will probably end up using our income to purchase the wrong things—goods that we do not value as much as other things that we might have bought.

Producers face costs too—the costs of the resources they use to make a product or provide a service. The use of resources such as lumber, steel, and sheet rock to build a new house, for example, takes resources away from the production of other goods, such as hospitals and schools. High production costs signal that the resources have other highly valued uses, as judged by buyers and sellers in other markets. Profit-seeking firms will heed those signals and act accordingly. However, government policies can override these signals with taxes or subsidies enacted to help those inconvenienced by changing prices in free and open markets. But such policies reduce the ability of market incentives to guide resources to where consumers ultimately, on balance, value them most highly.

Politicians and the lobbyists who seek their favors often speak of "free education," "free medical care," or "free housing." This terminology is deceptive. These things are not free. Scarce resources are required to produce each of them. The buildings, labor, and other resources used to produce schooling could, instead, produce more food or recreation or environmental protection or medical care. The cost of the schooling is the value of those goods that must now be given up. Governments may be able to shift costs, but they cannot avoid them.

With the passage of time, people often discover better ways of doing things and improve our knowledge of how to transform scarce resources into desired goods and services. During the last 250 years, economies with open markets have used this process to relax the grip of scarcity and improve their participants' quality of life. This has occurred to the greatest extent when and where the signals of open markets have been allowed to influence market participants, guiding their actions to the benefit of all, rather than those signals being defeated by politically potent groups seeking to avoid market discipline in order to enhance their own special interests.

3. Decisions Are Made at the Margin.

If we want to get the most out of our resources, we should undertake actions that generate more benefits than costs and refrain from actions that are more costly than they are worth. This principle of sound decision making applies to individuals, businesses, government officials, and society as a whole.

Nearly all choices are made at the margin. That means that they almost always involve additions to, or subtractions from, current conditions, rather than all-or-nothing decisions. The word "additional" is a substitute for "marginal." We might ask, "What is the marginal (or additional) cost of producing or purchasing one more unit?" Marginal decisions may involve large or small changes. The "one more unit" could be a new shirt, a new house, a new factory, or even an expenditure of time, as in the case of a high school student choosing among various activities. All these decisions are marginal because they involve additional costs and additional benefits.

We don't make all-or-nothing decisions, such as choosing between eating or wearing clothes—dining in the nude so we can buy lots of food. Instead we choose between having a little more food at the cost of a little less clothing or a little less of something else. In making decisions we don't compare the total value of food and the total value of clothing, but rather we compare their marginal values. A business executive planning to build a new factory will consider whether the marginal benefits of the new factory (for example, additional sales revenues) are greater than the marginal costs (the expense of constructing the new building). If not, the executive and his company are better off without the new factory.

Effective political actions will also reflect marginal decision making. Consider the political decision on how much effort should go into cleaning up pollution. If asked how much pollution we should allow, many people would respond none—in other words, we should reduce pollution to zero. In the voting booth they might vote that way. But marginal thinking reveals that this would be extraordinarily wasteful.

When there is a lot of pollution—so much, say, that we are choking on the air we breathe—the marginal benefit of reducing pollution is very high and is likely to outweigh the marginal cost of that reduction. But as the amount of pollution goes down, so does the marginal benefit—the value of the additional improvement in the air. There is still a benefit to an even cleaner atmosphere—for example, we will be able to see distant mountains—but this benefit is not nearly as valuable as saving us from choking. At some point before all pollution disappeared, the marginal benefit of eliminating more pollution would decline to almost zero.

But while the marginal benefit of reducing pollution is going down, the marginal cost is going up and becomes very high before all pollution is eliminated. The marginal cost is the value of other things that have to be sacrificed to reduce pollution a little bit more. Once the marginal cost of a cleaner atmosphere exceeds the marginal benefit, additional pollution reduction would be wasteful. It would simply not be worth the cost.

To continue with the pollution example, consider the following hypothetical situation. Assume that we know that pollution is doing $100 million worth of damage, and only $1 million is being spent to reduce pollution. Given this information, are we doing too little, or too much, to reduce pollution? Most people would say that we are spending too little. This may be correct, but it doesn't follow from the information given.

The $100 million in damage is total damage, and the $1 million in cost is the total cost of cleanup. To make an informed decision about what to do next, we need to know the marginal benefit of cleanup and the marginal cost of doing so. If spending another $10 on pollution reduction would reduce damage by more than $10, then we should spend more. The marginal benefit exceeds the marginal cost. But if an additional $10 spent on antipollution efforts would reduce damages by only a dollar, additional antipollution spending would be unwise.

People commonly ignore the implications of marginalism in their comments and votes but seldom in their personal actions. Consider food versus recreation. When viewed as a whole, food is far more valuable than recreation because it allows people to survive. When people are poor and living in impoverished countries, they devote most of their income to securing an adequate diet. They devote little time, if any, to playing golf, water skiing, or other recreational activities.

But as people become wealthier they can obtain food easily. Although food remains vital to life, continuing to spend most of their money on food would be foolish. At higher levels of affluence, they find that at the margin—as they make decisions about how to spend each additional dollar—food is worth much less than recreation. So as Americans become wealthier, they spend a smaller portion of their income on food and a larger portion of their income on recreation.[2]

The concept of marginalism reveals that it is the marginal costs and marginal benefits that are relevant to sound decision making. If we want to get the most out of our resources, we must undertake only actions that provide marginal benefits that are equal to or greater than marginal costs. Both individuals and nations will be more prosperous when the implications of marginalism are considered.

4. Trade Promotes Economic Progress.

The foundation of trade is mutual gain. People agree to an exchange because they expect it to improve their well-being. The motivation for trade is summed up in the statement: "If you do something good for me, I will do something good for you." Trade is productive because it permits each trading partner to get more of what he or she wants. There are three major sources of gains from trade.

First, trade moves goods from people who value them less to people who value them more. Trade increases the value obtained from goods even though nothing new is produced. When secondhand goods are traded at flea markets, through classified ads, or over the Internet, the exchanges do not increase the quantity of goods available (as new products do). But the trades move products toward people who value them more. Both the buyer and seller gain, or otherwise the exchange would not occur.

People's preferences, knowledge, and goals vary widely. A product that is virtually worthless to one person may be a precious gem to another. A highly technical book on electronics may be worth nothing to an art collector but valued at hundreds of dollars by an engineer. Similarly, a painting that an engineer cares little for may be cherished by an art collector. Voluntary exchange that moves the electronics book to the engineer and the painting to the art collector will increase the benefit derived from both goods. The trade will increase the wealth of both people and their nation. It is not just the amount of goods and services produced in a nation that determines the nation's wealth, but how those goods and services are allocated.

Second, trade makes larger outputs and consumption levels possible because it allows each of us to specialize more fully in the things that we do best. When people specialize in the production of goods and services that they can provide at a low cost, they can then sell these products to others and use the revenues to purchase items that would be costly for them to produce for themselves. Together, people who specialize this way will produce a larger total quantity of goods and services than would

14

otherwise be possible—and a combination of goods more varied and more desirable than they could have produced without specialization and trade. Economists refer to this principle as the law of comparative advantage. This law is universal: It applies to trade among individuals, businesses, regions, and nations.

The law of comparative advantage is just common sense. If someone else is able, and willing, to provide you with a product at a lower cost (keep in mind that all costs are opportunity costs) than you can provide it for yourself, it makes sense to trade for it. You can then use your time and resources to produce more of the things for which you are a low-cost producer. The result is that things are produced with less sacrifice of value than if people tried to produce most of the things they want for themselves, which would require people to produce things for which they don't have a comparative advantage.

For example, even though most doctors might be good at record keeping and arranging appointments, it is generally in their interest to hire someone to perform these services. The time doctors use to keep records is time they could have spent seeing patients. Because the time spent with their patients is worth a lot, the opportunity cost of doctors doing their own record keeping will be high. Thus, doctors will almost always find it advantageous to hire someone else to handle their record keeping. Moreover, when the doctor specializes in the provision of physician services and hires someone who has a comparative advantage in record keeping, costs will be lower and joint output larger than would otherwise be achievable.

Third, voluntary exchange allows firms to achieve lower per-unit costs by adopting large-scale production methods. Trade makes it possible for business firms to sell their output over a broad market area so they can plan for large outputs and adopt manufacturing processes that take advantage of economics of scale. Such processes often lead to substantially lower per-unit costs and enormous increases in output per worker. Without trade, these gains could not be achieved. Market forces are continuously reallocating production toward low-cost producers (and away from high-cost ones). As a result, open markets tend to allocate products and resources in ways that maximize the value, amount, and variety of the goods and services that are produced.

The importance of trade in our modern world cannot be exaggerated. Trade makes it possible for most of us to consume a bundle of goods and services far beyond what we would be able to produce for ourselves. Can you imagine the difficulty involved in producing your own housing, clothing, and food, to say nothing of computers, television sets, dishwashers, automobiles, and telephones? People who have these things do so largely because their economies are organized in such a way that individuals can cooperate, specialize, and trade. Countries that impose obstacles to exchange—either domestic or international—reduce the ability of their citizens to achieve gains from trade and more prosperous lives. Consider, for example, communist Cuba. Until 2008, citizens without political connections or government posts were prohibited from purchasing computers, cell phones, microwave ovens, and other luxury items.

5. Transaction Costs Are an Obstacle to Trade.

Voluntary exchange promotes cooperation and helps us get more of what we want. However, trade itself is costly. It takes time, effort, and other resources to search out potential trading partners, negotiate trades, and close the sale. Resources spent in this way are called transaction costs, and they are an obstacle to the creation of wealth. They limit both our productive capacity and the realization of gains from mutually advantageous trades.

Transaction costs are sometimes high because of physical obstacles, such as oceans, rivers, and mountains, which make it difficult to get products to customers. Investment in roads and improvements in transportation and communication can reduce these transaction costs. In other instances, transaction costs are high because of the lack of information. For example, you may want to buy a used copy of the economics book assigned for a class, but you don't know who has a copy and is willing to sell it at an attractive price. You have to try to find that person: The time and energy you spend doing so is part of your transaction costs.

Frequently transaction costs are high because of political obstacles, such as taxes, licensing requirements, government regulations, price controls, tariffs, or quotas. But regardless of whether the roadblocks are physical, informational, or political, high transaction costs reduce the potential gains from trade by diverting resources away from productive uses.

People who help others arrange trades and make better choices reduce transaction costs and promote economic progress. Such specialists, sometimes called middlemen, include campus bookstores, real estate agents, stockbrokers, automobile dealers, publishers of classified ads, and a wide variety of merchants.

Often people believe that these middlemen merely increase the price of goods and services without providing benefits. But once we recognize that transaction costs are an obstacle to trade, we can see the fallacy of this view. People often talk about eliminating the middleman, but they seldom do.

The grocer, for example, is a middleman. (Of course, today's giant supermarket reflects the actions of many people, but together their services are those of a middleman.) Think of the time and effort that would be involved in preparing even a single meal if shoppers had to deal directly with farmers when purchasing vegetables; citrus growers when buying fruit; dairy operators if they wanted butter, milk, or cheese; and ranchers or fishermen if they wanted to serve beef or fish. Grocers make these contacts for consumers, place the items in a convenient selling location, and maintain reliable inventories. The services of grocers and other middlemen reduce transaction costs significantly, making it easier for potential buyers and sellers to realize gains from trade. These services increase the volume of trade and promote economic progress.

6. Prices Bring the Choices of Buyers and Sellers into Balance.

Market prices will influence the choices of both buyers and sellers. When a rise in the price of a good makes it more expensive for buyers to purchase it, they will normally choose to buy fewer units. Thus, there is a negative relationship between the price of a good or service and the quantity demanded. This negative relation is known as the law of demand.

For sellers, the rise in the price of the product brings extra revenue that makes them more willing and able to supply more of it. Thus, there is a positive relationship between the price of a good and the quantity producers will supply. This positive relationship is known as the law of supply.

Economists often use graphics to illustrate the relationships among price, quantity demanded, and quantity supplied. When doing so, the price of a good is placed on the vertical y-axis and the quantity per unit time (e.g., week, month, or year) on the x-axis. Using milk as an example, Exhibit 1 illustrates the classic demand and supply graphic. The demand curve indicates the various quantities of milk consumers will purchase at alternative prices. Note how the demand curve slopes downward to the right, indicating that consumers will purchase more milk as its price declines. This is merely a graphic representation of the law of demand.

The supply curve indicates the various quantities milk producers are willing to supply at alternative prices. It slopes upward to the right, indicating that producers will be willing to supply larger quantities at higher prices. The supply curve provides a graphic representation of the law of supply.

Now for a really important point: The price will tend to move toward a level, $3 per gallon in our example, that will bring the quantity demanded into equality with the quantity supplied. At the equilibrium price of $3, consumers will want to purchase 15,000 gallons of milk per day, the same quantity that milk producers are willing to supply. Price coordinates the

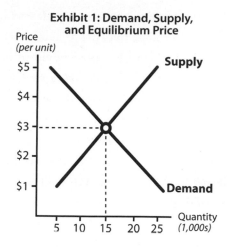

Exhibit 1: Demand, Supply, and Equilibrium Price

choices of both consumers and producers of milk and brings them into balance.

If the price is higher than $3—for example, $4—producers will want to supply more milk per day than consumers will want to purchase. At the $4 price, producers will be unable to sell as many units as they would like. Inventories will rise and this excess supply will lead some producers to cut their price to reduce their excess inventories. The price will tend to decline until the $3 equilibrium price is reached. It is easy to see, then, that if the price is above the equilibrium, market forces will push price down toward equilibrium.

Correspondingly, if the price of milk is less than $3, for example $2, consumers will want to purchase a larger quantity than producers are willing to supply. This generates excess demand and will place upward pressure on price; it will tend to move back toward the equilibrium of $3. The choices of buyers and sellers will be consistent with each other only at the equilibrium price and the market price will gravitate toward this level.

eBay illustrates the operation of demand and supply in a setting that is familiar to many. On eBay, sellers enter their reserve prices—the minimum prices they will accept for goods; buyers enter their maximum bids—the maximum prices they are willing to pay. The auction management system will bid on the buyers' behalf in predetermined monetary increments. Bidding ensues until the trading period expires or a person agrees to pay the stated "Buy-It-Now" price. Exchange occurs only when buyers bid a price greater than the seller's minimum asking price. But when this happens, an exchange will occur and both the buyer and seller will gain.

Though somewhat less visible than the eBay electronic market, the forces of demand and supply in other markets work similarly. The height of the demand curve indicates the maximum amount the consumer is willing to pay for another unit of the good, while the height of the supply curve shows the minimum price at which producers are willing to supply another unit. As long as the price is between the maximum the consumer is willing to pay and the minimum offer price of a seller, potential gains from trade are present. Moreover, when the equilibrium price is present, all potential gains from exchange will be realized.

Thus, consumers will tend to purchase only units that they value more than the actual price. Similarly, producers will supply only units that can be produced at a cost less than that price. When the equilibrium price is present, these conditions imply that units will be produced and purchased as long as the value of the good to consumers exceeds the cost of the resources required for its production. The implication: Market prices not only bring the quantity demanded and quantity supplied into balance, but they also direct producers to supply those goods that consumers value more highly than their cost of production. This holds true in any market.

Of course, we live in a dynamic world. Changes in factors like income, the price of substitute goods, and expected future price will alter the demand for goods. Similarly, changes in factors such as technology, resource prices, subsidies, and taxes will alter cost and the supply curve. Lower cost production methods will be discovered and new products introduced. However, if not restricted by price controls or other forms of political intervention, market prices will respond to dynamic changes and provide buyers and sellers with both the information and the incentive to bring their choices into harmony. These adjustments will not be instantaneous. It will take time for both consumers and producers to adjust fully to new conditions. Moreover, in a dynamic world, the adjustment process is continuous. As we proceed, we will analyze this process in more detail.[3]

7. Profits Direct Businesses Toward Activities That Increase Wealth.

The people of a nation will be better off if their resources—their land, buildings, labor, and entrepreneurial talent—produce valuable goods and services. At any given time a virtually unlimited number of potential investment projects are available to be undertaken. Some of these investments will increase the value of resources by transforming them into goods and services that consumers value highly relative to cost. These will promote economic progress. Other investments will reduce the value of resources and reduce economic progress. If we are going to get the most out of the available resources, projects that increase value must be encouraged, while those that use resources less productively must be discouraged.

This is precisely what profits and losses do. Business firms purchase resources (raw materials, intermediate goods, computers, software, machines, engineering and secretarial services, etc.) and use them to produce goods or services that are sold to consumers. If the sales of the products exceed the costs of all the resources required to produce them, then these firms profit. This means that profits result only if firms produce goods and services that consumers value more than the cost of the resources required for their production.

The value of a product to the consumer is measured by the price the consumer is willing to pay. If the consumer pays more than the production costs, then the decision by the producer to bid the resources away from their alternative uses was a profitable one. Profit is a reward for transforming resources into something of greater value.

In contrast, losses are a penalty imposed on businesses that produce goods and services that consumers value less than the resources required for their production. The losses indicate that the resources would have been better used producing other things.

Suppose it costs a shirt manufacturer $20,000 per month to lease a building, rent the required machines, and purchase the labor, cloth, buttons, and other materials necessary to produce and market one thousand shirts per month. If the manufacturer sells the thousand shirts for $22 each, he receives $22,000 in monthly revenue, or $2,000 in profit. The shirt manufacturer has created wealth—for himself and for the consumer. By their willingness to pay more than the costs of production, his customers reveal that they value the shirts more than they value the resources required for their production. The manufacturer's profit is a reward for increasing the value of resources by converting them into the more highly valued product.

On the other hand, if the shirts can be sold only for $17 each, then the manufacturer will earn $17,000, losing $3,000 a month. This loss occurs because the manufacturer's actions reduced the value of the resources. The shirts—the final product—were worth less to consumers than the value in other uses of the resources required for their production. We are not saying that consumers consciously know that the resources used to make the shirts would have been more valuable if converted into some other product. But their choices, taken together, reveal that fact, sending a clear message to the manufacturer, along with the incentive to reduce that loss by changing production plans.

In a market economy, losses and business failures work constantly to bring wasteful activities—such as producing shirts that sell for less than their cost—to a halt. Losses and business failures will redirect the resources toward the production of other goods that are valued more highly. Thus, even though business failures are often painful for the investors and employees involved, there is a positive side: They release resources that can be directed toward wealth-creating projects.

We live in a world of changing tastes and technology, imperfect knowledge, and uncertainty. Business owners cannot be sure what the future market prices will be or what the future costs of production will be. Their decisions are based on expectations. But the reward-penalty structure of a market economy is clear. Entrepreneurs who produce efficiently and who anticipate correctly the goods and services that attract consumers at prices above production cost will prosper. Business executives who allocate resources inefficiently, into areas where demand is weak, will be penalized with losses and financial difficulties.

Profits and losses direct business investment toward projects that promote economic progress and away from those that squander scarce resources. This is a vitally important function. Economies that fail to perform this function well will almost surely experience stagnation, or worse.

8. People Earn Income by Helping Others.

People differ in many ways—in their productive abilities, their preferences, their opportunities, their specialized skills, their willingness to take risks, and their luck. These differences influence people's incomes because they affect the value of the goods and services that individuals are willing and able to provide to others.

In a market economy, people who earn high incomes do so because they provide others with lots of things that they value. If these individuals did not provide valuable goods or services, consumers would not pay them so generously. There is a moral here: if you want to earn a high income, you had better figure out how to help others a great deal. To put that another way, if you are unable or unwilling to help others, your income will be low.

This direct link between helping others and receiving income gives each of us a strong incentive to acquire skills and develop talents so we can provide others with valuable goods and services. College students study for long hours, endure stress, and incur the financial cost of schooling in order to become doctors, chemists, accountants, and engineers. Other people acquire training, certification, and experience that will help them become electricians, maintenance workers, or computer programmers. Still others invest and start businesses. Why do people do these things?

In some cases individuals may be motivated by a strong personal desire to improve the world. However, and this is the key point, even people who don't care about improving the world, who are motivated mostly by the desire for income, will have a strong incentive to develop skills and take actions that are valuable to others. High earnings come from providing goods and services that others value. People seeking great wealth will have a strong incentive to pay close attention to what others want.

Some people think that high-income individuals must be exploiting others. But people who earn high incomes in the marketplace generally do so by improving the well-being of many people. Millions of people enjoy watching Oprah Winfrey's program, and she is rewarded with major earnings and other revenue from advertising endorsements. Céline Dion earns millions because many are willing to pay sizable amounts for her music. Business entrepreneurs who succeed in a big way do so by making their products affordable to millions of consumers. The late Sam Walton, who founded Walmart, became the richest man in the United States because he figured out how to manage large inventories effectively and sell brand-name merchandise at discount prices to small-town America. Bill Gates, the founder and chairman of Microsoft, rose to the top of the Forbes 400 list by developing a set of products that dramatically improved the efficiency and compatibility of desktop computers. Millions of consumers who never heard of either Walton or Gates benefited from their talents and low-priced products. Walton and Gates made a lot of money because they helped a lot of people.

9. Production of Goods and Services People Value, Not Just Jobs, Provides the Source of High Living Standards.

> *Consumption is the sole end and purpose of all production; and the interest of the producer ought to be attended to only so far as it may be necessary for promoting that of the consumer.*[4]
>
> —ADAM SMITH (1776)

As Adam Smith noted more than 230 years ago, consumption is the objective of all production. But goods and services cannot be consumed until they are produced. Moreover, income and living standards cannot increase without an increase in the availability of goods and services that people value.

Clearly, destroying commonly traded goods people value will make a society worse off. This proposition is so intuitively obvious that it almost seems silly to highlight it. But misguided politicians have often followed this course of action. In 1933, Congress passed the Agricultural Adjustment Act (AAA) in an effort to reduce supply and prevent the prices of agricultural products from falling. Under this New Deal legislation, the federal government paid farmers to plow under portions of their cotton, corn, wheat and other crops. Potato farmers were paid to spray their potatoes with dye so they would be unfit for human consumption. Healthy cattle, sheep, and pigs were slaughtered and buried in mass graves in order to keep them off the market. Six million baby pigs were killed under the AAA in 1933 alone. The Supreme Court declared the act unconstitutional in 1936, but not before it had kept millions of valuable agricultural products from American consumers. Moreover, under modified forms of the act, the government continues to pay various farmers to limit their production. While the political demands of those benefiting from the policies are understandable, such programs destroy valuable resources, making the nation poorer.

The 2009 Cash for Clunkers program provides another example of politicians attempting to promote prosperity by destroying productive assets—used cars, in this case. Under the Cash for Clunkers program, car dealers were paid between $3500 and $4500 to destroy the older cars that were traded in for a new automobile. Dealers were required to ruin the car engines with a sodium silicate solution, then smash them and send them to the junkyard, assuring that not even the parts would be available for future use. The proponents of this program argued that it would stimulate recovery by inducing people to buy new cars. But the money consumers used to buy new cars was unavailable for the purchase of other goods. Thus, while it temporarily stimulated auto purchases, it reduced spending in other areas. In essence, taxpayers provided $3 billion in subsidies for new car purchases, while destroying approximately 700,000 used cars valued at about $2 billion. New car sales plunged when the program expired and used cars became more expensive because of the reduction in their supply.

If destroying automobiles is a good idea, why not require owners to destroy their automobile every year? Think of all of the new car sales this would generate. All of this is crackpot economics. You may be able to help specific producers by making their products more scarce, but you cannot make the general populace better off by destroying marketable goods with consumption value.

A more subtle form of destruction involves government actions that increase the opportunity cost of obtaining various goods. For example, the federal government has subsidized the production of ethanol even though it costs about $1.50 more per gallon than the energy equivalent of gasoline. These subsidies increase our cost of obtaining energy and most also believe that they exert an adverse impact on the environment. But they help corn farmers in the important presidential primary state of Iowa, and therefore they will be difficult to repeal.

Politicians and proponents of government spending projects are fond of bragging about the jobs created by their spending programs and shamelessly exaggerate program benefits. Given this widespread deception, economic literacy in this area is particularly important. While employment is often used as a means to create wealth, we must not forget that it is not simply more jobs that improve our economic well-being but jobs that produce goods and services people value. When that elementary fact is forgotten, people are often duped into acceptance of programs that reduce wealth rather than create it.

The focus on jobs can be extremely misleading. This point is highlighted by the apocryphal story of an engineer who, while visiting China, came across a large crew of men building a dam with picks and shovels. When the engineer pointed out to the supervisor that the job could be completed in a few days, rather than many months, if the men were given motorized earthmoving equipment, the supervisor said that such equipment would destroy many jobs. "Oh," the engineer responded, "I thought you were interested in building a dam. If it's more jobs you want, why don't you have your men use spoons instead of shovels?"

Does government spending create jobs? When thinking about the answer to this question, consider the following two points. First, unless you believe in the tooth fairy, the funds for the spending will have to be either taxed or borrowed from the private sector. This will mean either higher taxes or higher interest rates, both of which will reduce private sector employment. This reduction in private employment will largely, if not entirely, offset the jobs generated by the government spending.

Second, the government spending itself will crowd out private spending and employment. When the government spends more on education, health care, charitable activities, and so on, households and businesses spend less. Similarly, when the government subsidizes some firms—for example, General Motors, Chrysler, Citigroup, or wind and solar energy producers—the subsidized firms will expand, but rival firms will lose market share and reduce their employment. Again, the increased government spending in one area will lead to offsetting reductions in employment in others.

The employment supported by the government spending can easily be seen, but the employment eliminated by the higher taxes, increased government borrowing, and reduction in demand for the products of the unsubsidized firms is largely unseen. This also helps to explain why deception is so widespread in this area. Nonetheless, the offsetting reductions in employment are real.

Remember how the so-called stimulus spending of both the Bush and Obama administrations was going to create and save millions of jobs? However, as the stimulus programs spent hundreds of billions of dollars during 2008–2009, employment fell and the unemployment rate soared. How could this be? Answer: As the government spent more, it crowded out private spending and therefore there was no net increase in employment. In fact, the programs generated uncertainty and probably made the situation worse.

The politicians supporting such programs, and those benefiting from the government spending, will not tell you about the offsetting reductions in private sector employment. Further, the fact that these programs do not utilize primarily voluntary trading, genuine market signals and incentives, and decisions by those personally facing the program costs gives us good reason to expect that the government-induced employment will be less productive than the private sector employment that it eliminates.

If a society is going to reach its potential, resources must be used to produce things people value more than the cost of their production. As previously discussed, profits and losses perform this function when resources are allocated by markets. The political process does not have anything like profit and loss that will consistently direct resources into productive, and away from counterproductive, projects. Worse still, when governments become heavily involved in granting favors to some at the expense of others, this incentive structure directs resources away from productive activities and toward the schmoozing of politicians (lobbying, high-paying jobs for those with political influence, and other forms of favor-seeking including bribery).

The use of taxpayer funds to grant businesses, labor unions, and other well-organized groups with subsidies and other forms of funding in exchange for political favors has become the major activity of government. This crony capitalism is not only reducing our income levels, it is corrupting the political process. Businesses and other interest groups continue to open offices in Washington, D.C., and more and more resources are directed toward the "looting" of the public treasury for private gain. Moreover, while the process reduces the living standards of ordinary Americans, the "looters" are doing quite well. It is no coincidence that the counties surrounding Washington now have the highest incomes of any in the country.

The bottom line is this: While consumption is the objective of all economic activity, goods and services must be produced before they can be consumed. When programs (1) destroy goods, (2) squander resources on projects that cost more than the value delivered to consumers, and (3) encourage individuals, businesses, and organized groups to enrich themselves at taxpayer expense, they will reduce both production and consumption, making us worse off as a society. When we analyze how the political process works in Part III, this issue will be considered in more detail.

10. Economic Progress Comes Primarily Through Trade, Investment, Better Ways of Doing Things, and Sound Economic Institutions.

On the first day of an introductory economics class, we often inform students that Americans produce and earn approximately thirty times as much per person today as in 1750. Then we solicit their views on the following question: "Why are Americans so much more productive today than they were two and a half centuries ago?" Think for a moment how you would respond to this question.

Invariably, our students mention three things: First, today's scientific knowledge and technological abilities are far beyond anything Americans imagined in 1750. Second, we have complex machines and factories, far better roads, and extensive systems of communication. Finally, students usually mention that in 1750 individuals and families directly produced most of the items that they consumed, whereas today we typically purchase them from others.

Basically, the students provide the correct explanation even though they have little or no prior knowledge of economics. They recognize the importance of technology, capital, and trade. Their response reinforces our view that economics is the science of common sense.

We have already highlighted gains from trade and the importance of reducing transaction costs as sources of economic progress. Economic analysis pinpoints three other sources of economic growth: investments in people and machines, improvements in technology, and improvements in economic organization.

First, investments in productive assets (tools and machines, for example) and in the skills of workers (investment in human capital) enhance our ability to produce goods and services. The two kinds of investment are linked. Workers can produce more if they work with more and better machines. A logger can produce more when working with a chain saw instead of a hand-operated, crosscut blade. Similarly, a transport worker can haul more with a truck than with a mule and wagon.

Second, improvements in technology (the use of brain power to discover new products and less costly methods of production) spur economic progress. Since 1750, the steam engine, followed by the internal combustion engine, electricity, and nuclear power replaced human and animal power as the major source of energy. Automobiles, buses, trains, and airplanes replaced the horse and buggy (and walking) as the chief methods of transportation. Technological improvements continue to change our lifestyles. Consider the impact of MP3 players, microcomputers, word processors, microwave ovens, video cameras, cell phones, DVDs, bypass surgery, hip replacements, automobile air conditioners, and even garage door openers. The introduction and development of these products during the last fifty years have vastly changed the way that we work, play, and entertain ourselves, and have improved our well-being.

Third, improvements in economic organization can promote growth. By economic organization we mean the ways that human activities are organized and the rules under which they operate—factors often taken for granted or overlooked. How difficult is it for people to engage in trade or to organize a business? The legal system of a country, to a large extent, determines the level of trade, investment, and economic cooperation undertaken by the residents of a nation. A legal system that protects individuals and their property, enforces contracts fairly, and settles disputes is an essential ingredient for economic progress. Without it, investment will be lacking, trade will be stifled, and the spread of innovative ideas will be retarded. Part II of this book will investigate in more detail the importance of the legal structure and other elements of economic organization.

Investment and improvements in technology do not just happen. They reflect the actions of entrepreneurs, people who take risks in the hope of profit. No one knows what the next innovative breakthrough will be or just which production techniques will reduce costs. Furthermore, entrepreneurs are often found in unexpected places. Thus, economic progress depends on a system that allows a very diverse set of people to try their ideas to see if they will pass the market test but also discourages them from squandering resources on unproductive projects.

For this progress to occur, markets must be open so that all are free to try their innovative ideas. An entrepreneur with a new product or technology needs to win the support of only enough investors to finance the project. But competition must be present so the entrepreneurs and their investors will be held accountable: Their ideas must face the "reality check" of consumers, who will decide whether or not to purchase a product or service at a price above the production cost. In this environment, consumers are the ultimate judge and jury. If they do not value an innovative product or service enough to cover its cost, it will not survive in the marketplace.

11. The "Invisible Hand" of Market Prices Directs Buyers and Sellers Toward Activities That Promote the General Welfare.

Every individual is continually exerting himself to find out the most advantageous employment for whatever capital he can command. It is his own advantage, indeed, and not that of the society which he has in view. But the study of his own advantage naturally, or rather necessarily, leads him to prefer that employment which is most advantageous to society. He intends only his own gain, and he is in this, as in many other cases, led by an invisible hand to promote an end which was not part of his intention.[5]

—ADAM SMITH (1776)

32

Self-interest is a powerful motivator. As Adam Smith noted long ago, when directed by the invisible hand, remarkably, self-interested individuals will have a strong incentive to undertake actions that promote the general prosperity of a community or nation. The invisible hand to which Smith refers is the prices determined by competitive markets. The individual "intends only his own gain," but he is directed by the invisible hand of market prices to promote the goals of others, leading to greater prosperity.

The principle of the invisible hand is difficult for many people to grasp. There is a natural tendency to associate order in a society with centralized planning. Yet Adam Smith contends that pursuing one's own advantage creates an orderly society in which demands are routinely satisfied without a central plan.

This order occurs because market prices coordinate the actions of self-interested individuals when private property and freedom of exchange are present. One statistic—the current market price of a particular good or service—provides buyers and sellers with what they need to know to bring their actions into harmony with the best possible information on the current actions and preferences of others. Market prices register the choices of millions of consumers, producers, and resource suppliers. They reflect information about consumer preferences, costs, and matters related to timing, location, and circumstances that in any large market are well beyond the comprehension of any individual or central-planning authority.

Have you ever thought about why the supermarkets in your community have approximately the right amount of milk, bread, vegetables, and other goods—an amount large enough that the goods are nearly always available but not so large that a lot gets spoiled or wasted? How is it that refrigerators, automobiles, and MP3 players, produced at diverse places around the world, are available in your local market in about the quantity that consumers desire? Where is the technical manual for businesses to follow to get this done? Of course there is no manual. The invisible hand of market prices provides the answer. It directs self-interested individuals into cooperative action and brings their choices into line with each other through price signaling as described in Element 6.

The 1974 Nobel Prize recipient Friedrich Hayek called the market system a "marvel" because just one indicator, the market price of a commodity, spontaneously carries so much information that it guides buyers and sellers to make decisions that help both obtain what they want.[6] The market price of a product reflects thousands, even millions, of decisions made around the world by people who don't know what the others are doing. For each commodity or service, the market acts like a giant computer network grinding out an indicator that gives all participants both the information they need and the incentive to act on it.

No individual or central-planning authority could possibly obtain or consider all the information needed for millions of consumers and producers of thousands of different goods and services to coordinate their actions the way markets do. Moreover, market prices contain this information in a distilled form. They will direct producers and resource suppliers toward production of those things that consumers value most (relative to their costs). No one will have to force a farmer to raise apples or tell a construction firm to build houses or convince a furniture manufacturer to produce chairs. When the prices of these and other products indicate that consumers value them as much or more than their production costs, producers seeking personal gain will supply them.

Nor will it be necessary for anyone to remind producers to search for and utilize low-cost methods of production. Self-interest directed by the invisible hand of market prices will provide them with a strong incentive to seek out the best combination of resources and the most cost-effective production methods. Because lower costs will mean higher profits, each producer will strive to keep costs down and quality up. In fact competition will virtually force them to do so.

In a modern economy, the cooperation that comes from self-interest directed by the invisible hand of market prices is truly amazing. The next time you sit down to a nice dinner, think about all the people who helped make it possible. It is unlikely that any of them, from the farmer to the truck driver to the grocer, was motivated by concern that you have an enjoyable meal at the lowest possible cost. Market prices, however, brought their interests into harmony with yours. Farmers who raise the best beef or turkeys receive higher prices, truck drivers and grocers earn more money if their products are delivered fresh and in good condition to the consumer, and so on, always using the low cost means to do so. Literally tens of thousands of people, most of whom we will never meet, make contributions that help each of us consume a bundle of goods that is far beyond what we could produce for ourselves. Moreover, the invisible hand works so quietly and automatically that the order, cooperation, and vast array of goods and services available to modern consumers are largely taken for granted. Even though underappreciated, the combination of self-interest and the invisible hand is nonetheless a powerful force for economic progress.

12. Too Often the Long-Term Consequences, or the Secondary Effects, of an Action Are Ignored.

Henry Hazlitt, an economics writer who began at the *Wall Street Journal* in 1913, was at the *New York Times* when his most famous book, *Economics in One Lesson,* was published in 1946. Hazlitt's one lesson was that when analyzing an economic proposal, a person:

> . . . *must trace not merely the immediate results but the results in the long run, not merely the primary consequences but the*

secondary consequences, and not merely the effects on some spe-cial group but the effects on everyone.[7]

Hazlitt believed that failure to apply this lesson was the most common source of economic error. He had written extensively on the economy during the Great Depression of the 1930s, and he knew that, especially in politics, there is a tendency to stress the short-term benefits of a policy while completely ignoring the longer-term consequences. When decisions are made politically, we hear an endless pleading for proposals to help specific industries, regions, or groups without consideration of how the proposal will impact the broader community, including taxpayers and consumers. Hazlitt clearly understood the basic postulates of economics and he also understood how the political system works.

Interest groups and the lobbyists hired to help them seek political fa-vors in the form of costly programs have an incentive to put the best spin on their case. They will exaggerate the benefits (most of which they will capture if the policy is enacted) and talk as if the costs (most of which will be borne by others) will be minimal. Such interest groups are most effec-tive if the benefits are immediate and easily visible to the voter, but the costs are less visible and mostly in the future. Under these conditions, interest groups can often mislead voters.

Thus voters often authorize actions that they would probably have re-jected if they had known the secondary effects or long-range consequences. Consider the case of rent controls imposed on apartments. Several large cities, including Newark, New York City, San Jose, and Washington, D.C., have adopted such controls, usually in response to claims that rent controls will keep rents from rising and make housing more affordable for the poor.

Yes, this is true in the short run, but there will be secondary effects. First, the market for apartments will stagnate. Existing apartments will not be transferred to those who want them most. For anyone to give up a rent-controlled apartment, even if another apartment is closer to work, will be costly to them, and it will be hard to find a closer one because others are holding on to theirs at the below-market rent.

The lower rental prices will also reduce investments in new housing. Although rent control may force current owners to accept a lower return, this will not be true for potential future owners. Because people respond to incentives, investors who would have put their funds into new apartments will channel them elsewhere. The number of rental units in the price-controlled area will decline, making it more difficult to find an apartment. Shortages will develop. Some people will have to commute longer distances to take advantage of lower prices and greater availability outside that area. The quality of rental housing will also fall with the passage of time because landlords receive little in return for maintenance; the shortage creates a demand for even poorly maintained units.

These secondary effects, however, will not be immediately observable. When the decline in the quality and quantity of apartments appears, many people will be puzzled about the cause. Thus, rent controls command substantial popularity, even though a declining supply of rental housing, poor maintenance, and shortages are the inevitable results. In the words of Swedish economist Assar Lindbeck: "In many cases rent control appears to be the most efficient technique presently known to destroy a city, except for bombing."[8]

Similarly, proponents of tariffs and quotas on foreign products almost always ignore the secondary effects of their policies. By limiting the importation of products from foreign countries, tariffs and quotas may initially protect the U.S. workers who make comparable products at a higher cost. But there will be secondary consequences, perhaps severe ones.

The steel import quotas imposed by the Bush administration in 2002 vividly illustrate this point. The quotas sharply reduced steel imports, and this reduction in supply pushed U.S. steel prices upward by about

30 percent. At the higher prices, the domestic producers of steel expanded both output and employment. But what about the secondary effects? The higher steel prices also made it more expensive to produce goods that contain a lot of steel, such as trucks, automobiles, and heavy appliances. American producers of these commodities were harmed by the quotas and often forced to lay off workers. American steel container producers, which had previously dominated the world market, sharply curtailed their employment because they were unable to compete with foreign firms purchasing steel at much lower prices.

Furthermore, there was an additional secondary effect. Because foreigners sold less steel in the U.S. market, they acquired fewer dollars with which to import American-made goods. Therefore, U.S. exports fell as a result of the import restrictions.

Once the secondary effects are considered, the impact on employment is clear: Trade restrictions do not create jobs; they reshuffle them. Employment may expand in industries shielded by quotas and tariffs, but it will contract in other industries, particularly export industries. The popularity of the restrictions is not surprising because the jobs of the people actually working in a shielded industry, steel in this case, are highly visible, while the secondary effects—the lost jobs in other industries— are less visible and difficult to trace back to the trade restrictions. Thus many people fall for the "protecting jobs" argument even though it is clearly fallacious when examined more closely.

Government spending also generates secondary effects that are often ignored. Politicians like to argue that government spending on favored projects expands employment. Of course there may be good reasons for government expenditures on roads, increased police protection, administration of justice, and so forth. The creation of jobs, however, is not one of them.

Suppose the government spends $50 billion on a project employing one million workers to build a high-speed train linking Los Angeles and

Las Vegas. How many jobs will the project create? Once the secondary effects are considered, the likely answer is none.

The reason is that the government must use either taxes or debt to finance the project. Taxes of $50 billion will reduce consumer spending and private savings, and this reduction will destroy as many jobs as the government spending will create. Alternatively, if the project is financed by debt, the borrowing will lead to higher interest rates and taxes to cover interest payments. This will divert funds away from other projects, both private and public.

The one million new jobs grab the headlines, but the loss of jobs in thousands of locations goes unrecognized. As in the case of trade restrictions, the result of this project is job rearrangement, not job creation. This fact does not necessarily mean that the project should not be undertaken. But it does mean that justification for the project must come from evidence that the benefits are greater than the costs of giving up other opportunities.

Secondary effects are not just a problem for governments and politicians. They can also lead to unanticipated outcomes for individuals. The recent experience of a first grade teacher in West Virginia illustrates this point. Her students were constantly losing their pencils, so she reasoned that if she paid them ten cents for the stub they would respond to the incentive to hang on to the pencil until it was all used. To her dismay, the students soon formed long lines at the pencil sharpener, creating stubs just as fast as she could pay for them. It pays to be alert for unintended consequences!

PART II

*Seven Major Sources
of Economic Progress*

SEVEN MAJOR SOURCES OF ECONOMIC PROGRESS

1. Legal system: The foundation for economic progress is a legal system that protects privately owned property and enforces contracts in an evenhanded manner.

2. Competitive markets: Competition promotes the efficient use of resources and provides a continuous stimulus for innovative improvements.

3. Limits on government regulation: Regulatory policies that reduce trade also retard economic progress.

4. An efficient capital market: To realize its potential, a nation must have a mechanism that channels capital into wealth-creating projects.

5. Monetary stability: A stable monetary policy is essential for the control of inflation, efficient allocation of investment, and achievement of economic stability.

6. Low tax rates: People will produce more when they are permitted to keep more of what they earn.

7. Free trade: A nation progresses by selling goods and services that it can produce at a relatively low cost and buying those that would be costly to produce domestically.

Introduction

Why do some countries grow rapidly, while others stagnate or even regress economically? Why are incomes per person so much higher in some countries than others?[1] Economists have asked these questions since Adam Smith's era in the eighteenth century. Capital investment and new technology clearly contribute to growth, but they do not take place in a vacuum. Countries must have certain characteristics that allow their people to interact productively. Sound institutions—the legal rules and customs, both formal and informal, that guide behavior—and sound government policies are the central elements of the growth process.

Just as one or two weak players can substantially reduce the overall performance of an athletic team, a counterproductive institution or policy in one or two key areas can substantially harm the performance of an economy. This section will discuss the major factors that underlie the growth process and explain why per capita incomes differ substantially across countries and time.[2]

1. Legal System: The Foundation for Economic Progress Is a Legal System That Protects Privately Owned Property and Enforces Contracts in an Evenhanded Manner.

[A] private property regime makes people responsible for their own actions in the realm of material goods. Such a system therefore ensures that people experience the consequences of their own acts. Property sets up fences, but it also surrounds us with mirrors, reflecting back upon us the consequences of our own behavior.[3]

—Tom Bethell

The legal system provides the foundation for the protection of property rights and enforcement of contracts. As we discussed in Element 4 of Part I, trade moves goods toward people who value them more and makes larger outputs possible as the result of gains from specialization and large-scale production methods. To reduce the uncertainties accompanying trade, a legal system must provide evenhanded enforcement of agreements or contracts. This will increase the volume of exchange and the gains from trade, and thereby promote economic progress.

The other critical role of the legal system is to protect property rights. Trade depends on property rights, and a legal system must protect property rights if an economy is to prosper. Property is a broad term that includes ownership of labor services and ideas, as well as physical assets such as buildings and land. Private ownership of property involves three things: (1) the right to exclusive use, (2) legal protection against invaders—those who would seek to use or abuse the property without the owner's permission—and (3) the right to transfer to (that is, exchange with) another.

Private owners can decide how they will use their property, and in turn, private owners are held accountable for their actions. People who use their property in a manner that invades or infringes on the property rights of another will be subject to the same legal forces that protect their own property. For example, private property rights prohibit me from throwing my hammer through the screen of your computer because if I did, I would be violating your property right to your computer. Your property right to your computer restricts me and everyone else from its use without your permission. Similarly, my ownership of my hammer and other possessions restricts you and everyone else from using them without my permission.

The important thing about private ownership is the incentives that flow from it. There are four major reasons why the incentives accompanying clearly defined and enforced private ownership rights propel economic progress.

First, private ownership encourages wise stewardship. If private owners fail to maintain their property or if they allow it to be abused or damaged, they will bear the consequences in the form of a decline in the property's value. For example, if you own an automobile, you have a strong incentive to change the oil, have the car serviced regularly, and see that the interior of the car is well maintained. Why is this so? If you are careless in these areas, the car's value to both you and potential future owners will decline. If the car is kept in good running order, it will be of greater value to you and to others who might want to buy it from you. For the owner, the market price will reflect that stewardship. Good stewardship is rewarded, but bad stewardship is penalized by a reduction in the value of the asset.

In contrast, when property is owned by the government or owned in common by a large group of people, the incentive for each user to take good care of it is weakened. For example, when the government owns housing, no individual or small group of owners has a strong financial incentive to maintain the property, because no individual or small group will pay the costs of a decline in the value of the property or benefit from its improvement. That is why government-owned housing, compared to privately owned housing, is more often run down and poorly maintained. This is true in both capitalist nations, where markets provide price signals, and in socialist countries, where they do not. Laxity in care, maintenance, and repair reflects the weak incentives that accompany government ownership of property, even in the midst of working markets.

Second, private ownership encourages people to use their property productively. When people are able to keep the fruits of their labor as private property, they have a strong incentive to improve their skills, work harder, and work smarter. Such actions will increase their income. Similarly, people will use their land, buildings, and other assets more productively when they are permitted to keep what they earn.

Farming in the former Soviet Union shows how property rights stimulate productive activity. Under the Communist regime, families were permitted to keep or sell the goods they produced on small private plots, which ranged up to an acre in size. These private plots made up only about 2 percent of the total land under cultivation; the other 98 percent consisted of huge, collectively owned farms where the land and the output belonged to the state. As reported by the Soviet press, approximately one-fourth of the total value of Soviet agricultural output was raised on that tiny fraction of privately farmed land. This indicates that the output per acre on the private plots was about sixteen times the per-acre output of the state-owned farms.

Even a modest move away from state ownership toward private ownership produces impressive results. In 1978 the Communist government of China began a de facto policy of letting farmers keep all rice grown on the collective farms over and above a specified amount that had to be given to the state. In effect the government turned a blind eye to farmers in the small village of Xiaogang in China's Anhui province. There, farmers began assigning responsibility for the cultivation of specific plots of land to particular farmers, with each farmer keeping all production above his contribution to the village's quota for the state. The result was an immediate increase in productivity. When the word got out, and the government ignored the official policy against such "privatization," the practice spread like wildfire, leading to rapid increases in agricultural output and freeing farmers to move into nonagricultural sectors of the economy. [4]

Third, private owners have a strong incentive to develop things that they own in ways that are beneficial to others. While private owners can legally do what they want with their property, they can gain from actions that enhance its value to others. If they employ and develop their property in ways that *others* find attractive, the market value of the property will increase. In contrast, changes that others dislike, particularly if the others are customers or potential future buyers, will reduce the value of one's property.

Consider the owner of an apartment complex who personally cares nothing about having parking spaces, convenient laundry facilities, a nice workout room, or an attractive lawn and swimming pool within the complex. If consumers value these things highly (relative to the costs of producing them) and other owners provide them, the owner has a strong incentive to provide them too. By making consumers better off, and thus willing to pay more, these features will enhance both the owner's earnings—the rents—and the market value of the apartments. In contrast, apartment owners who insist on providing only what they like, rather than the things that consumers prefer, will find that their earnings and the value of their capital (their apartments) are smaller.

Why are college students willing to endure long hours of study and incur the cost of a college education? Private ownership of labor services provides the answer. Because they have an ownership right to their labor services, their future earnings can be much greater if they acquire knowledge and develop skills that are highly valued by others.

Fourth, private ownership promotes the wise development and conservation of resources for the future. Using a resource may generate revenue. This revenue is the voice of *present* consumers, reflecting what they want from the resource. But *future* consumers, too, have a voice, thanks to property rights. An owner of a resource, say a woodlot or small forest, where the trees could be harvested now or later, may believe that the later harvest will be more valuable. In other words, the expected future value of the more mature trees, at the future price, will exceed their value if harvested now, by more than the cost of holding and protecting them for future use. The owner has an incentive to conserve—that is, hold back on current use—to make sure that the resource will be available when it is more valuable. In a sense the owner is heeding the voice of future consumers. Private owners can increase their personal wealth by balancing the demands in the present with the potential demand in the future.

Private owners gain by conservation whenever the expected future value of a consumable resource exceeds its current value. This is true even if the current owner does not expect to be around when the benefits accrue. Suppose that a sixty-five-year-old tree farmer is contemplating whether to cut his young Douglas fir trees. If the trees' growth and the increased scarcity of wood are expected to result in future revenues that exceed the current value of the trees, the farmer will gain by conserving the trees for the future. As long as ownership is transferable, the market value of the farmer's land will increase as the trees grow and the expected day of harvest moves closer. So even though the actual harvest may not take place until well after his death, the owner will be able to sell the trees (or, more likely, the land including the trees) at any time, capturing their increasing value.

For centuries pessimists have argued that we are about to run out of trees, critical minerals, or various sources of energy. Again and again they have been wrong because they failed to recognize the role of private property. It is instructive to reflect on these doomsday forecasts. In sixteenth-century England fear arose that the supply of wood—widely used as a source of energy—would soon be exhausted. Higher wood prices, however, encouraged conservation and led to the development of coal. The wood crisis soon dissipated.

Even when a specific resource is not owned, the market for other resources that *are* owned can often solve problems. In the middle of the nineteenth century, dire predictions arose that the United States was about to run out of whale oil, at the time the primary fuel for artificial lighting. No one owned the whales, which were being hunted to excess on the high seas. If a whale hunter failed to take a whale when the opportunity arose, someone else would probably do so in the near future. As whale oil prices rose, the incentive for individuals to conserve whales for the future was missing because private ownership rights were absent. No one limited whale hunting even though the whale population was declining. However, the higher whale oil prices did strengthen the incentive to find and develop substitute energy sources. If entrepreneurs could develop a cheaper new energy source, they could earn substantial revenues. With time this led to the development of relatively cheaper kerosene, a resulting drop in the price of whale oil, less whale hunting, and thus the end of the whale oil crisis.

Later, as people switched to petroleum, predictions emerged that this resource, too, would be exhausted. In 1914 the Bureau of Mines reported that the total U.S. supply of oil was under six billion barrels, about what the United States now produces every 40 months. In 1926 the Federal Oil Conservation Board estimated that the U.S. supply of oil would last only seven years. A couple of decades later the Secretary of the Interior forecast that the United States would run out of oil in just a few more years. A study sponsored by the Club of Rome made similar predictions for the world during the 1970s.

Understanding the incentives that emanate from private ownership makes it easy to see why doomsday forecasts have been so wrong. When the scarcity of a privately owned resource increases, the price of the resource will rise. The increase in price provides consumers, producers, innovators, and engineers with an incentive to (1) conserve on the direct use of the resource, (2) search more diligently for substitutes, and (3) develop new methods of discovering and recovering larger amounts of the resource. To date these forces have pushed doomsday ever farther into the future, and there is every reason to believe that they will continue to do so for resources that are privately owned.[5]

Over time, this process of conservation, substitution, and new technology can keep resources available for many generations—and it can also allow a multitude of resources to come into play. For example, although oil and natural gas have displaced coal in many uses, the United States still uses coal for almost 50 percent of its electricity production, and we have massive reserves still in the ground. We have more energy options than ever before. If the current energy prices should skyrocket, we will see entrepreneurs heighten their efforts to develop economical ways to harness wind, solar power, and nuclear energy. Similarly, if regulations that have protected some buyers against competition from others, or some sellers against competition from others, are relaxed and competition is thus increased, we can expect more efforts to economize on the use of costly resources, along with more efforts to produce more of those resources that are now revealed to be more valuable to society.

A legal system that protects property rights and enforces contracts in an evenhanded manner provides the foundation for capital formation and gains from trade, which are the mainsprings of economic growth. In contrast, insecure property rights, uncertain enforcement of agreements, and legal favoritism undermine both investment and gains from trade. Throughout history people have tried other forms of ownership such as large-scale cooperatives, socialism, and communism. On any scale beyond the small village with a strong cultural harmony, these experiences have ranged from unsuccessful to disastrous. To date we do not know of any institutional arrangement that provides individuals with as much freedom and incentive to serve others by using resources productively and efficiently as does private ownership within the framework of the rule of law.

2. Competitive Markets: Competition Promotes the Efficient Use of Resources and Provides a Continuous Stimulus for Innovative Improvements.

> *Competition is conducive to the continuous improvements of indus-*
> *trial efficiency. It leads producers to eliminate wastes and cut costs*
> *so that they may undersell others. It weeds out those whose costs re-*
> *main high and thus operates to concentrate production in the hands*
> *of those whose costs are low.*[6]
>
> —CLAIR WILCOX

Competition is present when the market is open and alternative sellers are free to enter and compete. Competition is the lifeblood of a market economy. The rival firms may compete in local, regional, national, or even global markets. The competitive process places pressure on each producer to operate efficiently and cater to the preferences of consumers. Competition weeds out inefficient producers. Firms that fail to provide consumers with quality goods at competitive prices will experience losses and eventually be driven out of business. Successful competitors have to outperform rival firms. They may do so through a variety of methods, including quality of product, style, service, convenience of location, advertising, and price, but they must consistently offer consumers at least as much value relative to cost as rivals make available.

What keeps McDonald's, Walmart, General Motors, or any other business firm from raising prices, selling shoddy products, and providing lousy service? Competition provides the answer. If McDonald's fails to provide a tasty sandwich at an attractive price delivered with a smile, people will turn to Burger King, Wendy's, Subway, Taco Bell, and other rivals. Even the largest firms will lose business to small upstarts that find ways to provide consumers with better products at lower prices. For example, when Walmart was nothing more than a few small stores in Arkansas, Sears was a retailing giant. Now, Walmart is the world's largest retailer with sales that dwarf those of Sears. Firms as large as Toyota, General Motors, and Ford will lose customers to Honda, Hyundai, Volkswagen, and other automobile manufacturers if they fall even a step behind in providing the type of vehicle people want at competitive prices.

Competition gives firms a strong incentive to develop better products and discover lower-cost methods of production. Because technology and prices change constantly, no one knows precisely what products consumers will want next or which production techniques will minimize costs per unit. Competition helps discover the answer. Is Internet marketing the greatest retail idea since the shopping mall? Or is it simply another dream that will eventually turn to vapor? Competition will provide the answer, which will differ across markets and change over time.

In a market economy entrepreneurs are free to innovate. They need only the support of investors (often including themselves) willing to put up the necessary funds. The approval of central planners, a legislative majority, or business rivals is not required. Nonetheless, competition holds entrepreneurs and the investors who support them accountable because their ideas must face a reality check imposed by consumers. If consumers value the innovation enough to cover its costs, the new business will profit and prosper. But if consumers find that the new product is worth less than it costs, the business will suffer losses and fail. Consumers are the ultimate judge and jury of business innovation and performance.

Producers who wish to survive in a competitive environment cannot be complacent. Today's successful product may not pass tomorrow's competitive test. In order to succeed in a competitive market, businesses must be good at anticipating, identifying, and quickly adopting improved ideas.

Competition also discovers the business structure and size of firm that can best keep the per-unit cost of a product or service low. Unlike other economic systems, a market economy does not mandate the types of firms that are permitted to compete. Any form of business organization is permissible. An owner-operated firm, partnership, corporation, employee-owned firm, consumer cooperative, commune, or any other form of business is free to enter the market. To succeed it has to pass only one test: cost-effectiveness. If a business entity, whether a corporation or an employee-owned firm, produces quality products at attractive prices, it will profit and succeed. But if its structure results in higher costs than other forms of business organization, competition will drive it from the market.

The same point is true for the size of a firm. Companies that manufacture airplanes and autos, for example, must be quite large to take full advantage of economies of scale. Building a single automobile would be extremely costly, but when the fixed costs are spread over many thousands of units, the costs of producing each car can plummet. Naturally, consumers will tend to buy from the firms that can produce goods economically and sell them at lower prices. In such industries, most small firms will eventually be driven from the market.

In other instances, however, small firms, often organized as individual proprietorships or partnerships, will be more cost-effective. When consumers place a high value on personalized service and individualized products, large firms may have a hard time competing. Thus law and medical practices, printing shops, and hair-styling salons are usually small firms. A market economy permits cost considerations and the interaction between producers and consumers to determine the type and size of firm.

Competition is not pro-business. Businesses do not like to face competition and commonly lobby for policies to protect themselves from it. However, the competition that keeps profit rates low will also persistently direct businesses toward entrepreneurial actions that result in better goods and services at lower costs. In contrast, government regulations that limit entry into markets and favor some businesses over others undermine the competitive process and retard economic progress.

Competition harnesses personal self-interest and puts it to work elevating our society's standard of living. As Adam Smith noted in *The Wealth of Nations:*

> *It is not from the benevolence of the butcher, the brewer, or the baker that we expect our dinner, but from their regard to their own self-interest. We address ourselves not to their humanity but to their self-love, and never talk to them of our own necessities, but of their advantages.*[7]

Paradoxical as it may seem, self-interest directed by competition is a powerful force for economic progress. Dynamic competition among products, technologies, organizational methods, and business firms will weed out the inefficient and consistently lead to the discovery and introduction of superior products and technologies. When the new methods improve quality and/or reduce costs, they will grow rapidly and often replace the old ways of doing things. History abounds with examples. The automobile replaces the horse and buggy. The supermarket replaces the mom-and-pop grocery store. Fast-food chains like McDonald's and Wendy's expand and largely replace the local diner. Walmart and Target grow rapidly while other retailers contract and firms like Ward's are driven from the market. MP3s and iPods replace CD players, which had previously displaced cassette decks and record players. Personal computers replace typewriters, and smart phones substitute for some PCs. One could go on and on with similar examples. The great economist Joseph Schumpeter referred to this dynamic competition as creative destruction, and he argued that it formed the very core of economic progress. He was right.

3. Limits on Government Regulation: Regulatory Policies That Reduce Trade Also Retard Economic Progress.

As we previously noted, trade promotes social gain—a larger output and more income than would be otherwise achievable. When governments limit cooperation through trade, they stifle economic progress. Governments reduce trade in three ways.

First, many countries impose regulations that limit entry into various businesses and occupations. In those countries, if you want to start a business or provide a service, you have to acquire a license, fill out forms, get permission from different bureaus, show that you are qualified, indicate that you have sufficient financing, and meet various other regulatory tests. Some officials may refuse your application unless you are willing to pay a bribe or contribute to their political coffers. Often, well-established and politically influential businesses that you would be competing against can successfully oppose your application.

Hernando de Soto, in his revealing book *The Mystery of Capital*, reports that in Lima, Peru, it took 289 days for a team of people working six hours a day to meet the regulations required to legally open a small business producing garments. (In an earlier book, *The Other Path,* he revealed that along the way, ten bribes were solicited and it was necessary to pay two of the requested bribes in order to get permission to operate legally.) A 2009 publication of the World Bank reported that, given current regulations, legally opening a business would take 196 days in Haiti, 155 days in the Democratic Republic of Congo, 152 days in Brazil, and 141 days in Venezuela. By way of comparison, opening this same business would take only 4 days in Singapore, 6 in the United States, and 11 in Hong Kong.[8] A business financed with foreign capital often faces an additional maze of regulations. Regulations that make it costly to legally operate a business stifle competition, encourage political corruption, and drive decent people into the underground (or what de Soto calls the informal) economy.

Second, regulations that substitute political authority for the rule of law and freedom of contract will tend to undermine gains from trade. Several countries make a habit of adopting laws that grant political administrators substantial discretionary authority. For example, in the mid-1980s, customs officials in Guatemala were permitted to waive tariffs if they thought that doing so was in the "national interest." Such legislation is an open invitation for government officials to solicit bribes. It creates regulatory uncertainty and makes business activity more costly and less attractive, particularly for honest people. The law needs to be precise, unambiguous, and nondiscriminatory. If it is not, it will be a major roadblock to gains from trade.

Regulatory roadblocks are costly to the economy and to most individuals, but of course regulations do help some businesses by restricting competitors. Because such regulations are lucrative to the few who benefit, they impose an additional cost: business, labor and other special-interest groups will seek advantage for their constituents by trying to influence the political process. Some will lobby politicians and regulators to establish or increase these roadblocks, while others (those most severely harmed) will lobby to diminish their effects. Lobbying for all sides of any issue consumes the time and effort of highly skilled individuals, plus costs of travel, entertainment, publishing, advertising, and other activities.

Many countries have imposed regulations that interfere with and undermine the use of contracts or voluntary agreements to deal with various issues. This has been particularly true in the labor market. Minimum-wage legislation, forcing collective bargaining agreements on nonconsenting parties, and employee dismissal regulations substitute government regulations for contractual agreements. A number of European countries require employers who want to reduce the size of their workforce to (1) obtain permission from political authorities, (2) notify the dismissed employees months in advance, and (3) continue paying the dismissed employees for several more months.

These regulations may appear to be in the interests of workers, but the secondary effects must be considered. Regulations that make it costly to dismiss workers also make it costly to hire them; employers will be reluctant to take on additional workers because of the costs they will have to incur. As a result, the growth of employment in countries that impose extensive labor market regulations will be stifled. It will be very difficult for new labor force entrants to find jobs; and high unemployment rates, particularly for workers under age thirty-five, will result. Indeed, the restrictive labor market regulations of most Western European countries are the primary reason why their unemployment rates have been 4 or 5 percentage points higher than the United States during the past couple of decades. [9]

Third, the imposition of price controls will also stifle trade. Governments sometimes set prices above the market level; for example, they may require a minimum price for milk or gasoline. These prices lead buyers to purchase fewer units than they otherwise would. Governments also set prices lower than the market level, as in cases of apartment rent controls and regulated electric power rates. These prices make suppliers unwilling to produce as much. In terms of units produced and sold, it makes little difference whether price controls push prices up or force them down; both will reduce the volume of trade and the gains from production and exchange.

Exchange is productive; it helps us get more from the available resources. Regulatory policies that force traders to pass through various political roadblocks are almost always counterproductive. A country cannot realize its full potential unless restrictions that limit trade and increase the cost of doing business are kept to a minimum. For those who value liberty and prosperity, the market is the best regulator.

4. An Efficient Capital Market: To Realize Its Potential, a Nation Must Have a Mechanism That Channels Capital into Wealth-Creating Projects.

While consumption is the goal of all production, it will often be more economical to use resources to build machines, heavy equipment, and buildings that can then be used to produce the desired consumer goods. Capital investment (the construction and development of long-lasting resources designed to help us produce more in the future) is an important potential source of economic growth.

Resources (such as labor, land, and entrepreneurship) used to produce these investment goods will be unavailable for the production of consumer goods. If we consume all that we produce, no resources will be available for investment. Therefore, investment requires savings (giving up current consumption). Someone (either the investor or someone willing to supply funds to the investor) must save in order to finance investment. Saving is an integral part of the investment process.

Not all investment projects, however, are productive. An investment project will enhance the wealth of a nation only if the value of the additional output derived from the investment exceeds the cost of the investment. When it does not, the project is counterproductive and reduces wealth. Investments can never be made with perfect foresight, so even the most promising investment projects will sometimes fail to enhance wealth. To make the most of its potential for economic progress, a nation must have a mechanism that will attract savings and channel them into the investments that are most likely to create wealth.

In a market economy, the capital market performs this function. The capital market, when defined broadly, includes the markets for stocks, real estate, and businesses, as well as loanable funds. Financial institutions such as stock exchanges, banks, insurance companies, mutual funds, and investment firms play important roles in the operation of the capital market.

Private investors, such as small-business owners, corporate stockholders, and venture capitalists, place their own funds at risk in the capital market. Investors will sometimes make mistakes; sometimes they will undertake projects that prove to be unprofitable. If investors were unwilling to take such chances, many new ideas would go untested and many worthwhile but risky projects would not be undertaken.

The development of the Internet illustrates the interaction among entrepreneurship, risk-taking, and the capital market. Two Stanford University graduate students, Sergey Brin and Larry Page, would have seemed unlikely candidates for entrepreneurial success as they worked on a research project in the mid-1990s. In 1998, they founded Google, Inc., a business providing free Internet services that generates revenues through advertising. The powerful Internet search engine Brin and Page developed increases the productivity of millions of individuals and businesses each day. They have earned a fortune and Google is a household name with about 20,000 employees. Other Internet-based companies, such as eBay and Amazon, have also earned profits and achieved growth and success during the past decade. But the experience of numerous others was quite different. Many dot-coms, like Broadband Sports and eVineyard, went bust because their revenues were insufficient to cover their costs. The high hopes of these firms did not pan out.

In a world of uncertainty, mistaken investments are a necessary price that must be paid for fruitful innovations in new technologies and products. Such counterproductive projects, however, must be recognized and brought to a halt. In a market economy, the capital market performs this function. If a firm continues to experience losses, eventually investors will terminate the project and stop wasting their money.

Given the pace of change and the diversity of entrepreneurial talent, the knowledge required for sound decision-making about the allocation of capital is far beyond the scope of any single leader, industrial planning committee, or government agency. Without a private capital market, there is no mechanism that can be counted on to consistently channel investment funds into wealth-creating projects.

When investment funds are allocated by the government, rather than by the market, an entirely different set of factors comes into play. Political influence rather than market returns will decide which projects will be undertaken. Predictably, investment projects that reduce rather than create wealth will become far more likely.

The experiences of Eastern Europe and the former Soviet Union illustrate this point. For four decades (1950–90), the investment rates in these countries were among the highest in the world. Central planners allocated approximately one-third of the national output into capital investment. Even these high rates of investment, however, did little to improve living standards because political rather than economic considerations determined which projects would be funded. Resources were often wasted on politically impractical projects and high visibility ("prestige") investments favored by important political leaders. Misdirection of investment and failure to keep up with dynamic change eventually led to the collapse of these systems.

Recent U.S. experience with government allocation of credit for housing finance also illustrates how political allocation of capital works. The Federal National Mortgage Association and Federal Home Loan Mortgage Corporation, commonly known as Fannie Mae and Freddie Mac, were chartered by Congress as government-sponsored corporations in 1968 and 1970, respectively. It was thought that they would improve the operation of the capital market and make home financing more affordable. While Fannie Mae and Freddie Mac were privately owned "for profit" businesses, their government sponsorship meant that investors perceived that their bonds were less risky. Therefore, Fannie and Freddie were able to borrow funds at approximately half of a percentage point cheaper than private firms. This gave them a huge advantage over their rivals and they were highly profitable for many years.

But the government sponsorship also made Fannie Mae and Freddie Mac highly political. The President appointed several members to their board of directors. Top management of Fannie and Freddie provided key congressional leaders with large political contributions and often hired away congressional staffers into high-paying jobs lobbying their former bosses. Their lobbying activities were legendary. Between 1998 and 2008, Fannie Mae spent $79.5 million and Freddie Mac spent $94.9 million lobbying Congress for special favors and continuation of their privileged status.[10]

Fannie Mae and Freddie Mac did not originate mortgages. Instead, they purchased them in the secondary market, a market where mortgages originated by banks and other lenders are purchased. Propelled by their cheaper access to funds, by the mid-1990s, these two government-sponsored enterprises held approximately 40 percent of all home mortgages. Their dominance of the secondary market was even greater. During the decade prior to their insolvency in 2008, Fannie Mae and Freddie Mac purchased more than 80 percent of the mortgages sold by banks and other mortgage originators.

Responding to earlier congressional directives, the Department of Housing and Urban Development mandated that, by 1996, 40 percent of the mortgages financed by Fannie Mae and Freddie Mac must go to households with incomes below the median. This figure was increased to 50 percent by 2000 and to 56 percent by 2008. In order to meet these mandates, Fannie and Freddie began accepting more mortgages with little or no down payment. They also substantially increased their mortgages to subprime borrowers, those with a poor credit history. Because of their dominance of the secondary market, their lending practices exerted a huge impact on the lending standards accepted by mortgage originators. Recognizing that riskier loans could be passed on to Fannie and Freddie, the originators had less incentive to scrutinize the creditworthiness of borrowers or worry much about their ability to repay the funds. After all, sale of the mortgage to Fannie and Freddie would transfer the risk to them as well.

As Exhibit 2 shows, subprime mortgages (including those extended with incomplete documentation) soared from 4.5 percent of the new mortgages in 1994 to 13.2 percent in 2000 and to nearly one-third of the total share of mortgage originations by 2005–2006. During the same time frame, conventional loans, for which borrowers are required to make at least a 20 percent down payment, fell by a similar percentage. The default and foreclosure rates for subprime loans range from seven to ten times the parallel rates for conventional loans to prime borrowers. Predictably, the growing share of loans to those with weaker credit would eventually lead to higher default and foreclosure rates.

Both Congress and the administrations of Bill Clinton and George W. Bush were highly supportive of these regulatory policies and took credit for the initial increase in home ownership they helped to generate. As the policies eroded mortgage-lending standards, making credit more readily available for risky loans, the initial effects seemed positive. The demand for housing increased, housing prices soared during 2001–2005, and there was a boom in the construction industry.

But the artificially created boom was not sustainable. By 2004–2005, approximately half of all mortgages were either subprime (including those with incomplete documentation) or loans against the equity people had in their homes with the higher and still rising home price levels. As soon as prices leveled off and then began to decline during the second half of 2006, the house of cards came crashing down. The mortgage default and foreclosure rates immediately began to rise. All of this occurred

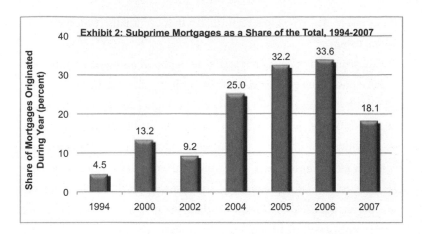

Source: The 1994–2000 data are from Edward M. Gramlich, *Financial Services Roundtable Annual Housing Policy Meeting*, Chicago, Illinois, 21 May 2004. The 2002–2007 data are from the Joint Center for Housing Studies of Harvard University, *The State of the Nations Housing 2008*, http://www.jchs.harvard.edu/son/index.htm. Loans with incomplete documentation and verification, known as Alt-A loans, are included in the subprime category. Studies indicate that most of the Alt-A loans were to subprime borrowers.

well before the recession, which did not start until December 2007. Of course the collapse of the housing industry eventually spread to the rest of the economy, and the bad mortgages generated huge financial problems in banking and finance both in the U.S. and abroad. By summer 2008, Fannie Mae and Freddie Mac were insolvent. Their operations were totally taken over by the government and the American taxpayer was left with at least $400 billion of bad debt.

The interest rate policies of the Federal Reserve System (Fed) were also a major contributing factor to the Great Recession of 2008, as we will explain in the following element. But one thing is clear: The political allocation of credit and the regulatory erosion of lending standards channeled a lot of financial capital into projects that should never have been undertaken. Many home buyers were incentivized to purchase more housing than they could afford; this was a major contributing factor in the boom-bust cycle in the housing industry that eventually resulted in a severe recession.[11]

When property rights are clearly defined and enforced, competitive markets direct entrepreneurs toward projects that are both profitable and wealth enhancing. Rising incomes and higher living standards are a natural result. In contrast, when capital is allocated by government officials, political objectives become more important and considerations of economic efficiency less so. Politicians will be more interested in how the investments will affect the special interest groups that help them flex their political muscles and improve their prospects of winning the next election. They will be less focused on whether the investments are productive in a lasting way.

Historically, the governments in other countries have generally played a larger role in the allocation of investment than the government of the United States has. When governments are heavily involved, allocation of investment is inevitably characterized by side payments, favoritism, bribes, and other forms of corruption. When actions of this type occur in other countries, they are often referred to as crony capitalism. Regardless of the label, political allocation of capital imposes a heavy cost on citizens. The American experience with government allocation of investment funds for housing is consistent with this view.

5. Monetary Stability: A Stable Monetary Policy Is Essential for the Control of Inflation, Efficient Allocation of Investment, and Achievement of Economic Stability.

Money is vitally important for the operation of an economy. First and foremost, money is a means of exchange. It reduces transaction costs because it provides a common denominator into which the value of all goods and services can be converted. Money also makes it possible for people to gain from complex exchanges with a time dimension, such as the sale or purchase of a home or car, that involve the receipt of income or payment of a purchase price across lengthy time periods. And it provides us with a means to store purchasing power for future use. Money is also a unit of accounting that enhances our ability to keep track of benefits and costs, including those incurred across time periods.

The productive contribution of money, however, is directly related to the stability of its value. In this respect, money is to an economy what language is to communication. Without words that have clearly defined meanings to both speaker and listener, communication is impossible. So it is with money. If money does not have a stable and predictable value, it will be difficult for borrowers and lenders to find mutually agreeable terms for a loan; saving and investing will involve additional risks; and time-dimension transactions (such as payment for a house or automobile over time) will be fraught with additional uncertainty. When the value of money is unstable, many potentially beneficial exchanges are not made and the gains from specialization, large-scale production, and social cooperation are reduced.

There is no mystery about the cause of monetary instability. Like other commodities, the value of money is determined by supply and demand. When the supply of money is constant or increases at a slow, steady rate, the purchasing power of money will be relatively stable. In contrast, when the supply of money expands rapidly compared to the supply of goods and services, the value of money declines and prices rise. This is inflation. It occurs when governments print money or borrow from a central bank in order to pay their bills.[12]

Politicians often blame inflation on such scapegoats as greedy businesses, powerful labor unions, big oil companies, or foreigners. But this is a ruse—a diversionary tactic. Persistent inflation has a single source: rapid growth in the supply of money. A nation's money supply is its currency, checking accounts, and traveler's checks. When that supply increases faster than the growth of the economy, the result is inflation.

Exhibit 3 illustrates the linkage between growth of the money supply

Exhibit 3: Monetary Growth and Inflation, 1990–2007		
	Annual Growth Rate of the Money Supply (%)	Avg Annual Growth Rate of Inflation (%)
Slow Growth of the Money Supply		
United States	2.1	2.8
Central African Republic	2.3	3.4
Singapore	2.5	1.4
New Zealand	2.8	2.1
Sweden	4.0	2.0
Maritius	4.7	6.5
Canada	5.1	2.1
Rapid Growth of the Money Supply		
Peru	22.7	21.9
Uruguay	24.6	23.9
Ghana	24.8	22.2
Malawi	27.4	23.8
Nigeria	27.5	21.9
Romania	35.6	61.7
Venezuela	36.8	32.9
Hypergrowth of the Money Supply		
Turkey	71.8	51.6
Ukraine	84.5	89.9
Congo, Dem. Rep.	140.3	360.4
Zimbabwe	164.8	165.3

Source: The World Bank, *World Development Indicators, 2009* and International Monetary Fund, *International Financial Statistics* (annual). The growth rate of the money supply is measured by the nominal growth of the money supply minus the growth of the real gross domestic product (GDP). The data for the Ukraine are for 1992–2007.

and inflation. Note how countries that increased their money supply at a slow rate (5 percent or less) experienced low rates of inflation during 1990–2007. This was true for large high-income countries like the United States and Canada, as well as for smaller ones like Singapore, New Zealand, and Sweden. It was also true for poor countries like the Central African Republic and Mauritius.

As the money supply of a country grew faster, however, so too did the rate of inflation (see data for Peru, Uruguay, Ghana, Malawi, Nigeria,

Romania, and Venezuela). The money supply in these countries grew at an annual rate of between 20 percent and 40 percent, and most experienced annual inflation rates in the same range. Extremely high rates of monetary growth (70 percent and above) led to hyperinflation, as in Turkey, Ukraine, the Democratic Republic of the Congo and Zimbabwe. As the growth rate of the money supply in these countries soared, so too did their rate of inflation.

Every country in the world with a low inflation rate in recent decades has had a policy of slow monetary growth. Conversely, every country that has experienced rapid inflation has followed a course of rapid monetary expansion. Historically, this link between rapid monetary growth and inflation has been one of the most consistent relationships in all of economics.

High and variable rates of inflation undermine prosperity. When prices increase 20 percent one year, 50 percent the next year, 15 percent the year after that, and so on, individuals and businesses are unable to develop sensible long-term plans. The uncertainty makes the planning and implementation of capital investment projects risky and less attractive. Unexpected changes in the inflation rate can quickly turn an otherwise profitable project into a personal economic disaster. Rather than dealing with these uncertainties, many decision makers will simply forgo capital investments and other transactions involving long-term commitments. Some will even move their business and investment activities to countries with a more stable environment. As a result, potential gains from trade, business activities, and capital formation will be lost.

Moreover, when governments inflate, people will spend less time producing and more time trying to protect their wealth. Because failure to accurately anticipate the rate of inflation can devastate one's wealth, individuals will shift scarce resources away from the production of goods and services and toward actions designed to hedge against inflation. The ability of business decision makers to forecast changes in prices becomes more valuable than their ability to manage and organize production. When the inflation rate is uncertain, businesses will shy away from entering into long-term contracts, place many investment projects on hold, and divert resources and time into less productive activities. Funds will flow into the purchase of gold, silver, and art objects, in the hope that their prices will rise with inflation, rather than into more productive investments such as buildings, machines, and technological research. As resources move from more productive to less productive activities, economic progress slows.

Inflation also undermines the credibility of government. At the most basic level, people expect government to protect their persons and property from intruders who would take what does not belong to them. But the government becomes an intruder when it cheats citizens in the same way that counterfeiters do by creating money, spending it, and watering down its value. How can people have any confidence that the government will protect their property against other intrusions, enforce contracts, or punish unethical and criminal behavior? When the government degrades its own currency, it is in a weak position to punish, for example, an orange juice producer who dilutes juice sold to customers or a business that waters down its stock (that is, issues additional stock without permission of current stockholders).

Economic progress will also be undermined when monetary policy makers are constantly shifting between monetary expansion and contraction. When the monetary authorities expand the money supply rapidly, initially the more expansionary monetary policy will generally push interest rates to a low level, which will stimulate current investment and generate an artificial economic boom. The low interest rates will attract investment into projects that appear to be profitable, but will not be sustainable for very long. When the expansionary monetary policy continues, it will generate inflation, which will cause monetary policy makers to shift toward a more restrictive policy. However, as they do so, interest rates will rise, which will retard private investment and throw the economy into a recession. Thus, monetary shifts from expansion to restriction will generate economic instability. The economy will be jerked back and forth between booms and busts. This pattern of monetary policy will also create uncertainty, retard private investment, and reduce the rate of economic growth.

This is exactly what happened during 1968–1982 in the United States. The monetary authorities followed an expansionary policy that fueled inflation and, as the inflation rate rose, the policy makers shifted toward restriction, which threw the economy into a recession. The recessions of 1970, 1974–1975, 1980, and 1982 were primarily the result of the "speedup and slowdown" monetary policy of this era.

More recently, expansionary monetary policy pushed short-term interest rates to historic low levels during 2002–2004, as policy makers sought to stimulate a more rapid recovery from the recession of 2001. As Exhibit 4 shows, the 1-year Treasury bill interest rate was maintained at 2 percent or less throughout 2002, 2003, and 2004. This expansionary monetary policy, coupled with the regulations that eroded lending standards discussed in the previous element, generated a housing market boom. However, as the inflation rate rose during 2005, the Fed shifted to a more restrictive monetary policy and interest rates rose. This retarded the housing price inflation, but it also soon led to soaring mortgage default and housing foreclosure rates, and eventually to the Great Recession of 2008.[13]

The combination of regulations promoting loose mortgage lending standards and the Fed's artificially low interest rate policies encouraged decision makers to borrow more money and make housing investments beyond what they could afford. While the policy created a housing construction boom during 2002–2005, many of these investments were uneconomical. They should never have been undertaken. They comprise what economists call mal-investment. Before an economy can return to a

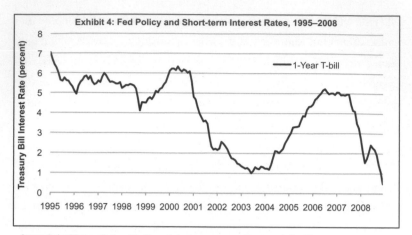

Source: Federal Reserve System, http://www.federalreserve.gov, and Economagic, http://www.economagic.com

sustainable path of growth, these badly allocated investments will have to be cleansed from the system. As the severe contraction during 2007–2009 illustrates, this is a costly and painful process.

Monetary stability is an essential ingredient of the environment for economic progress. Without monetary stability, potential gains from capital investment and other exchanges involving time commitments will be eroded and the people of the country will fail to realize their full potential.

The keys to monetary stability are (1) growth of money and credit consistent with price stability and (2) avoidance of "speedup and slowdown" policy shifts in response to current economic conditions. As Milton Friedman noted several decades ago, inflation is caused by excessive money growth. Rapid money growth will lead to inflation. Moreover, changes in monetary policy will impact prices, output, and employment with lengthy and unpredictable time lags.[14] Thus, attempts to manipulate real output and employment through persistent shifts in monetary policy will generate instability rather than stability. Modern monetary policy makers appear to understand the link between money growth and inflation. However, as the

U.S. monetary policy of the past decade indicates, they still have insufficient awareness of the damage done by "speedup and slowdown" monetary policies.

6. Low Tax Rates: People Will Produce More When They Are Permitted to Keep More of What They Earn.

Taxes are paid in the sweat of every man who labors. If those taxes are excessive, they are reflected in idle factories, in tax-sold farms, and in hordes of hungry people tramping streets and seeking jobs in vain.

—FRANKLIN D. ROOSEVELT, OCTOBER 19, 1932

When high tax rates take a large share of income, the incentive to work and use resources productively declines. The marginal tax rate is particularly important. This is the share of additional income that is taxed away at any given income level. For example, in the United States in 2009, if a taxpayer with $50,000 in taxable income earned an extra $100, he or she had to pay $25 of that $100 in federal income tax. The taxpayer faced a marginal tax rate of 25 percent. As marginal tax rates increase, the share of additional earnings that individuals are permitted to keep goes down.

There are three reasons why high marginal tax rates will reduce output and income.

First, high tax rates discourage work effort and reduce the productivity of labor. When marginal tax rates soar to 55 or 60 percent, individuals get to keep less than half of their additional earnings. When people are not allowed to keep much of what they earn, they tend not to earn very much. Some, perhaps people with working spouses, will drop out of the labor force to work at home, where their work is not taxed. Others will simply work fewer hours, retire earlier, or take jobs with longer vacations or a more preferred location. Still others will be more particular about accepting jobs when unemployed, refuse to move to take a job or to gain a pay raise, or forget about pursuing that promising but risky business venture. High tax rates can even drive a nation's most productive citizens to countries where taxes are lower. These substitutions will reduce the size and productivity of the available labor supply, causing output to decline.

Of course, most people will not immediately quit work, or even work less diligently, in response to an increase in the marginal tax rate. A person who has spent years training for a particular occupation will probably continue working—and working hard—especially if that person is in the peak earning years of life. But many younger people who have not already made costly investments in specialized training will be discouraged from doing so by high marginal tax rates. Thus some of the negative effects of high tax rates on work effort will be felt as reduced productivity for many years in the future.

High tax rates will reduce productivity and gains from trade in other ways, too. Employment taxes (or payroll taxes) drive a wedge between the employer's cost of hiring a worker and the employee's take-home pay. The employer pays more to employ this worker than the worker receives in pay. As this gap becomes larger, employment will decline as the cost of hiring increases and some workers leave the workforce or even shift to the underground economy, where legal protections are less certain and property rights less secure. In those markets, both labor and capital are less productive for the society as a whole.

High tax rates will also cause some to shift to activities in which they are less productive because they do not have to pay taxes on them. For example, high taxes will drive up the costs of skilled painters, perhaps leading you to paint your own house, even though you lack the skill to do it efficiently. Without high tax rates, the professional painter would do the job at a cost you could afford, and you could spend your time doing work for which you are better suited. Waste and economic inefficiency result from these tax-distorted incentives.

Second, high tax rates will reduce both the level and efficiency of capital formation. High tax rates repel foreign investment and cause domestic investors to search for investment projects abroad where both taxes and production costs are relatively lower, compared to the higher-tax situation at home. This reduces investment and the availability of productive equipment, which provide the fuel for economic growth. Domestic investors will also turn to projects that shelter current income from taxation and away from projects with a higher rate of return but fewer tax-avoidance benefits. These tax shelters enable people to gain personally from projects that do not enhance the value of resources. Scarce capital is wasted, and resources are channeled away from their most productive uses.

Third, high marginal tax rates encourage individuals to consume tax-deductible goods in place of nondeductible goods, even though the nondeductible goods may be more desirable. When purchases are tax deductible, individuals who purchase them do not bear their full cost, because the expenditure reduces the taxes they would otherwise pay. When marginal tax rates are high, tax-deductible expenditures become relatively cheap.

The sales of the British-made luxury car, Rolls-Royce, in the 1970s provides a vivid illustration of this point. The marginal income tax rates in the United Kingdom were as high as 98 percent on high earners during this era. A business owner paying that tax rate could buy a car as a tax-deductible business expense, so why not buy an exotic, more expensive car? The purchase would reduce the owner's profit by the car's price—say £100,000—but the owner would have received only £2,000 of the profit anyway, because of the 98 percent marginal tax rate. In effect, the government was paying 98 percent of the car's costs (mirrored in lost tax revenue from that decision). When the UK cut the top marginal tax rate to 70 percent, the sales of Rolls-Royces fell dramatically. After the rate reduction, the £100,000 car now cost the business owner not £2,000 but £30,000. The lower marginal rates made it much more expensive for wealthy Brits to purchase Rolls-Royces and other super-luxury cars, and they responded by reducing their purchases.

High marginal rates artificially reduce the personal cost, *but not the cost to society,* of items that are tax deductible, or that can be taken as a business expense. Predictably, taxpayers confronting high marginal tax rates will spend more money on such tax-deductible items as plush offices, Hawaiian business conferences, business entertainment, and a company-provided automobile. Because such tax-deductible expenditures reduce their taxes, people will often buy goods they would not buy if they were paying for the full cost. Waste and inefficiency are by-products of high marginal tax rates and the perverse incentive structure they generate.

Reductions in tax rates, particularly high rates, can increase the incentive to earn and improve the efficiency of resource use. The United States has had three major reductions in tax rates: the rate reductions during the 1920s in the aftermath of World War I, the Kennedy tax cuts of the 1960s, and the Reagan tax cuts of the 1980s. All were followed by strong and lengthy expansions in real output.

In contrast, large tax increases can exert a disastrous impact on the economy. The tax policy during the Great Depression clearly illustrates this point. Seeking to reduce the federal budget deficit in 1932, the Republican Hoover administration and the Democratic Congress passed the largest peacetime tax rate increase in the history of the United States. The lowest marginal tax rate on personal income was raised from 1.5 percent to 4 percent. At the top of the income scale, the highest marginal tax rate was raised from 25 percent to 63 percent. Essentially, personal income tax rates were more than doubled in one year! This huge tax increase reduced the aftertax income of households and the incentive to earn, consume, save, and invest. The results were catastrophic. In 1932, real output fell by 13 percent, the largest single-year decline during the Great Depression era. Unemployment rose from 15.9 percent in 1931 to 23.6 percent in 1932.

Just four years later, the Roosevelt administration increased taxes again, pushing the top marginal rate to 79 percent in 1936. Thus, during the latter half of the 1930s, high earners were permitted to keep only 21 cents of each additional dollar they earned. (Note: It is interesting to contrast the words of candidate Roosevelt presented at the top of this element with the tax policy followed during his presidency.) Several other factors, including a huge contraction in the money supply and a large increase in tariff rates, contributed to both the severity and the length of the Great Depression. But it is also clear that the tax increases of both the Hoover and Roosevelt administrations played a major role in this tragic chapter of American history.[15]

In summary, economic analysis indicates that high tax rates will reduce productive activity, retard capital formation, and promote wasteful use of resources. They are an obstacle to prosperity and the growth of income. Moreover, large tax rate increases during a period of economic weakness can exert a disastrous impact on the economy.

7. Free Trade: A Nation Progresses by Selling Goods and Services That It Can Produce at a Relatively Low Cost and Buying Those That Would Be Costly to Produce Domestically.

Free trade consists simply in letting people buy and sell as they want to buy and sell. Protective tariffs are as much applications of force as are blockading squadrons, and their objective is the same—to prevent trade. The difference between the two is that blockading squadrons

*are a means whereby nations seek to prevent their enemies from
trading; protective tariffs are a means whereby nations attempt to
prevent their own people from trading.*[16]

—HENRY GEORGE

The principles involved in international trade are basically the same as
those underlying any voluntary exchange. As is the case with domestic
trade, international trade makes it possible for each of the trading partners to produce and consume more goods and services than would otherwise be possible. There are three reasons why this is so.

***First, the people of each nation benefit if they can acquire a product
or service through trade more cheaply than they can produce it domestically.*** Resource endowments differ substantially across countries. Goods
that are costly to produce in one country may be economical to produce in
another. For example, countries with warm, moist climates such as Brazil
and Colombia find it advantageous to specialize in the production of coffee. People in Canada and Australia, where land is abundant and population sparse, tend to specialize in land-intensive products, such as wheat,
feed grains, and beef. The citizens of Japan, where land is scarce and the
labor force highly skilled, specialize in manufacturing such items as cameras, automobiles, and electronic products for export. Trade will permit
each of the trading partners to use more of their resources to produce and
sell things they do well rather than having them tied up producing things
at a high cost. As a result of this specialization and trade, total output increases and people in each country are able to achieve a higher standard of
living than would otherwise be attainable.

***Second, international trade allows domestic producers and con-
sumers to benefit from the economies of scale typical of many large operations.*** This point is particularly important for small countries. With

international trade, domestic producers can operate on a larger scale and therefore achieve lower per-unit costs than would be possible if they were solely dependent on their domestic market. Trade makes it possible for the textile manufacturers of China, Mexico, and South Korea to enjoy the fruits of large-scale production. If they were unable to sell abroad, their costs per unit would be much higher because their domestic textile markets are too small to support large, low-cost firms in this industry. With international trade, however, textile firms in these countries are able to produce and sell large quantities and compete effectively in the world market.

International trade also allows domestic consumers to benefit by purchasing from large-scale producers abroad. Given the huge design and engineering costs of planes today, for example, no country has a domestic market large enough to permit even a single airplane manufacturer to realize fully the economies derived from large-scale production. With international trade, however, Boeing and Airbus can sell many more planes, each at a lower cost. As a result, consumers in every nation can fly in planes purchased economically from such large-scale producers.

Third, international trade promotes competition in domestic markets and allows consumers to purchase a wider variety of goods at lower prices. Competition from abroad keeps domestic producers on their toes. It forces them to improve the quality of their products and keep costs down. At the same time, the variety of goods available from abroad provides consumers with a much greater array of choices than would be available without international trade.

Governments often impose regulations that restrain trade. These can be tariffs (taxes on imported goods), quotas (limits on the amount imported), exchange rate controls (artificially holding down the value of the domestic currency to discourage imports and encourage exports), or bureaucratic regulations on importers or exporters. All increase transaction costs and reduce the gains from exchange. As Henry George noted in the quote above, trade restraints are like a military blockade that a nation imposes on its own people. Just as a blockade imposed by an enemy will harm a nation, imposing a blockade in the form of trade restrictions also harms the nation.

Noneconomists often argue that import restrictions can create jobs. As we discussed in Part I, Element 9, it is production of value that really matters, not jobs. If jobs were the key to high incomes, we could easily create as many as we wanted. All of us could work one day digging holes and the next day filling them up. We would all be employed, but we would also be exceedingly poor because such jobs would not generate goods and services that people value.

If we are going to achieve higher living standards, we must expand the availability of the things people value. Trade helps us do so. When residents are permitted to trade with whomever they want, domestic consumers can find the lowest prices and the most value from their expenditures. Similarly, domestic producers can sell their goods and services wherever they can command the highest prices. As a result, consumers get more for their money, and we are able to produce a larger output from the available resources. It is this expansion in production and consumption, not just jobs, that underlies higher income levels and living standards.

Import restrictions may appear to expand employment because the industries shielded by restraints may increase in size or at least remain steady. This does not mean, however, that the restrictions expand total employment. Remember the secondary effects discussed in Part I, Element 12. When Americans erect tariffs, quotas, and other barriers limiting the ability of foreigners to sell in the United States, this will simultaneously limit the ability of foreigners to buy goods and services produced in the United States. Our imports provide foreigners with the purchasing power they need to buy our exports. If foreigners are unable to sell as much to Americans, they will have fewer of the dollars required to buy from Americans.

Thus import restrictions will indirectly reduce exports. Output and employment in export industries will decline, offsetting any jobs "saved" in the protected industries.[17]

Trade restrictions neither create nor destroy jobs; they reshuffle them.[18] The restrictions artificially direct workers and other resources toward the production of things that we produce at a high cost compared to others. Output and employment shrink in areas where our resources are more productive—areas where our firms could compete successfully in the world market if it were not for the side effects of the restrictions. Thus labor and other resources are shifted away from areas where their productivity is high and moved into areas where it is low. Such policies reduce both the output and income levels of Americans.

Many Americans believe that U.S. workers cannot compete with foreigners who sometimes make as little as $2 or $3 per day. This fallacious view stems from a misunderstanding of both the source of high wages and the law of comparative advantage. Workers in the United States are well educated, possess a high skill level, and work with large amounts of capital equipment. These factors contribute to their high productivity, and their high productivity is the source of their high wages. In low-wage countries like Mexico and China, wages are low precisely because productivity is low.

Each country will always have some things that it does relatively better than others. Both high- and low-wage countries will benefit when they can focus on using more of their resources pursuing productive activities that they do comparatively well. If a high-wage country can import a product from foreign producers at a price lower than the price of producing it domestically, importing it makes sense. Fewer of our resources will be tied up producing items that could be supplied domestically only at a high cost and more will be directed toward production of things that we do well—goods and services that domestic producers can supply at a low cost.[19] Trade will make it possible for workers in both high and low wage countries to produce a larger output than would otherwise be possible. In turn, the higher level of productivity will lead to higher wages for both.

High wages and living standards result from high productivity, not jobs. The French economist Frédéric Bastiat dramatically illustrated this point in his 1845 satire, "A Petition on Behalf of the Candlestick Makers." The petition was supposedly written to the French Chamber of Deputies by French producers of candles, lanterns, and other products providing indoor lighting. The petition began by complaining that domestic suppliers of light were "suffering from the ruinous competition of a foreign rival who apparently works under conditions so superior to our own for production of light that he is *flooding* the *domestic market* with it at an incredibly low price; for the moment he appears, our sales cease, all the consumers turn to him, and a branch of the French industry whose ramifications are innumerable is all at once reduced to complete stagnation." Of course this rival is the sun, and the petitioners are requesting that the Deputies "pass a law requiring the closing of all windows, inside and outside shutters, . . . , and blinds—in short, all openings, holes, chinks, and fissures through which the light of the sun is wont to enter houses." The petition goes on to list the occupations in the lighting industry in which there would be a large increase in employment if the use of the sun for indoor lighting was outlawed. And this direct expansion in employment would increase incomes that would be spent, and thus expand employment throughout the country to the benefit of all. Bastiat's point in this satire is obvious. As silly as the proposed legislation in the petition is, it is no sillier than legislation that reduces the availability of low-cost goods and services in order to "save" domestic producers and promote employment.[20]

Another way to look at the "saving jobs" issue is to consider that if trade restraints are a good idea, we should favor tariffs and quotas limiting trade among the states of the United States. It is true that, for example, Nebraska loses (or fails to get) specific kinds of jobs when it purchases oranges from Florida, winter vegetables from California, and cotton from Texas. All of these products could be produced in Nebraska, but only at a high cost. Thus, Nebraskans generally find it cheaper to "import" these commodities rather than produce them locally. Nebraska gains by using its resources to produce and "export" corn, wheat, livestock, and other goods. The profits generated through their "export" sales provide the purchasing power for people from Nebraska to "import" goods of greater variety and at far less cost than they could produce them locally.

Indeed, most people recognize that free trade among the fifty states is a major source of prosperity for each of the states. Imports from other states do not destroy jobs; they merely release workers for employment in export industries, where they will be able to produce more value and therefore generate more income at lower cost. If free trade among the fifty states promotes prosperity, so too will free trade among nations.

The proponents of trade restrictions may well believe that their policies will be good for the economy. But, as we have stressed before, good intentions provide little protection from the consequences of bad policy. The Smoot-Hawley tariff bill of 1930 provides a vivid illustration. By mid-April of 1930, the stock market had increased for five straight months and had rebounded to the level just prior to the October 1929 crash. At that point, serious congressional debate on the Smoot-Hawley tariff bill began, the legislation moved through Congress, and it was signed into law on June 17, 1930.

President Herbert Hoover, Senator Reed Smoot, Congressman Willis Hawley, and other proponents of the bill thought higher tariffs would stimulate the economy and save jobs. As Hawley put it, "I want to see American workers employed producing American goods for American consumption."[21]

The results were just the opposite. The bill increased tariffs by more than 50 percent on approximately 3,200 imported products. This surge in taxes on imports angered foreigners and sixty countries responded with higher tariffs on American products. International trade plunged and so did output in the United States. By 1932 the volume of U.S. trade had fallen to less than half its earlier level. Gains from trade were lost, the tariff revenues of the federal government actually fell, output and employment plunged, and the unemployment rate soared. Unemployment stood at 7.8 percent when the Smoot-Hawley bill was passed, but it ballooned to 23.6 percent of the labor force just two years later. The stock market, which had been above 280 at passage, fell below 90 in the two years following its passage.

More than a thousand economists signed an open letter to President Hoover warning of the harmful effects of Smoot-Hawley and pleading with him not to sign the legislation. He rejected their pleas, but history confirmed the validity of their warnings. Other factors, such as the sharp contraction in the money supply and the huge tax increases of both 1932 and 1936, contributed to the Great Depression. But the Smoot-Hawley tariff bill was also a major cause of the tragic events of that era.[22]

Why do so many countries adopt trade restrictions? Economic illiteracy on the part of both voters and policy makers plays a role. But there is another crucially important factor here: the political power of organized special interests. Trade restrictions benefit particular producers and their resource suppliers, including some workers, at the expense of consumers and suppliers to other industries. Usually a specific industry that wants the government to provide them with protection from foreign rivals will be well organized and highly visible, while consumers, other workers, and other resource suppliers are generally poorly organized and their gains from international trade more widely dispersed. Predictably, the organized interest group will deliver more political clout, more votes, and more campaign funds; many politicians will cater to their views.

Furthermore, the harm to the workers who lose their jobs when steel, for example, can be produced more cheaply abroad and freely imported is easily visible. The harm to the workers in other industries who lose their jobs (or take less productive jobs) due to tariffs is not easily traced back to the tariffs and generally goes unnoticed. In the case of trade restrictions, sound economic thinking often conflicts with a winning political strategy.

But this does not change the reality of the situation. Expansion of world trade has made more and more goods and services available at economical prices. The poor, in particular, have benefited from the freer trade. Worldwide, several hundred million poor people have moved out of poverty during the past quarter of a century. Residents of the United States have also benefited. International trade is a good example of how we improve our own well-being by helping others improve theirs.

We should present the case for free trade to other countries, but just because others are employing harmful policies, it does not follow that we should. To the contrary, the United States would gain substantially if it unilaterally phased out all of its trade restrictions over, for example, a ten-year period. Such an action would improve the well-being of Americans and, at the same time, improve economic conditions around the world. Moreover, there is also reason to believe that removal of our trade restrictions would help promote peace. While there is no magic bullet that can eliminate either war or terrorism, trade does expand the opportunities for people to achieve better lives through productive activities rather than destructive ones. In that regard, more trade will be at least a modest step toward a more peaceful world.

The Importance of Institutions and Policies: Concluding Thoughts

How much do institutions and policies matter? In order to answer this question, we need a way of comparing the institutions and policies of different countries. In the mid-1980s, the Fraser Institute of Vancouver, British Columbia, began work on a special project designed to develop a cross-country measure of economic freedom. Several leading scholars, including Nobel laureates Milton Friedman, Gary Becker, and Douglass

North, participated in the endeavor. This project culminated with the development of the Economic Freedom of the World (EFW) index.[23] Now published by a worldwide network of 75 institutes, this index measures the extent to which a country's institutions and policies are consistent with economic freedom; that is, with personal choice, private ownership, voluntary exchange, and competitive markets. The index incorporates 42 separate components and provides ratings for approximately one hundred countries throughout the 1980–2007 period.

In many ways the EFW index reflects the elements of economic progress outlined above. To achieve a high EFW rating, a country must provide secure protection of privately owned property, evenhanded enforcement of contracts, and a stable monetary environment. It also must keep taxes low, refrain from creating barriers to both domestic and international trade, and rely more fully on markets rather than government expenditures and regulations to allocate goods and resources. If these institutional and policy factors really do affect economic performance, countries with persistently high EFW ratings should do much better than those with persistently low ratings.

Exhibit 5 presents data on the 2007 per capita income and its growth for the ten countries with the highest and lowest EFW ratings during 1990–2007. Among the ninety-nine countries and jurisdictions for which the EFW data were available over the almost-two-decade period, Hong Kong, Singapore, New Zealand, and the United States headed the list of the most persistently free economies. At the other end of the spectrum, Guinea-Bissau, the Democratic Republic of the Congo, Zimbabwe, and Algeria were the least free economies. The average per capita income of the ten most free economies was $37,412, almost thirteen times the figure ($2,920) for the ten least free economies. Not only did the ten most free economies have a substantially higher income level, they also grew more rapidly. The growth rate of the ten most free economies averaged

Exhibit 5: Economic Freedom, Per Capita GDP

	EFW Rating, 1990–2007	GDP Per Capita 2007 PPP (constant 2005 international $)	Growth Rate of Per Capita GDP 1990–2007 PPP (percent, constant 2005 international $)
10 Highest Rated Countries, 1990–2007			
Hong Kong	8.8	$39,958	3.1
Singapore	8.6	$47,497	4.1
New Zealand	8.2	$25,282	1.9
United States	8.2	$43,102	1.8
Switzerland	8.1	$37,581	0.7
United Kingdom	8.0	$33,717	2.1
Canada	7.9	$36,260	1.8
Ireland	7.8	$41,036	5.1
Australia	7.7	$32,735	2.0
Netherlands	7.7	$36,956	2.0
Average	**8.1**	**$37,412**	**2.5**
10 Lowest Rated Countries, 1990–2007			
Niger	5.0	$597	−0.7
Burundi	5.0	$349	−1.9
Venezuela	4.9	$11,480	1.1
Syria	4.9	$4,038	1.9
Central Afr. Rep.	4.8	$674	−1.0
Congo, Rep. of	4.8	$3,517	0.1
Algeria	4.7	$7,317	1.0
Zimbabwe*	4.4	$450	−1.6
Congo, Dem. Rep.	4.2	$288	−4.3
Guinea-Bissau	4.2	$495	−2.1
Average	**3.9**	**$2,920**	**−0.8**

Source: Derived from World Bank, *World Development Indicators,* and James Gwartney and Robert Lawson, *Economic Freedom of the World: 2009 Annual Report.*

* *1990 to 2005 GDP data are used for Zimbabwe because the data is unavailable for 2006 and 2007. Myanmar was in the original bottom ten but it is omitted here because the GDP data are unavailable.*

2.5 percent annually during 1990–2007, compared to negative 0.8 percent for the ten least free economies.

Exhibits 6a and 6b break the 99 countries into quartiles arrayed from low to high by their EFW rating and then presents data for the average income level and growth rate for each of the four groups. The same pattern emerges: the freer economies among the ninety-nine both achieve higher per capita income levels and grow more rapidly.[24] The most free

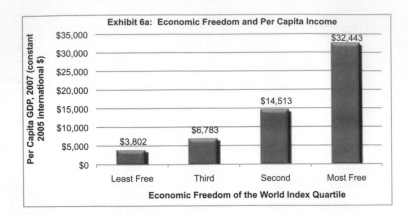

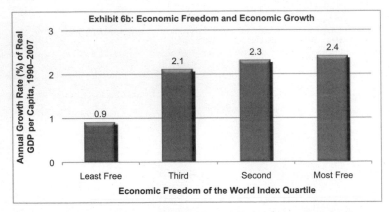

Source: Derived from World Bank, *World Development Indicators*, and James Gwartney and Robert Lawson, *Economic Freedom of the World, 2009 Annual Report.*

countries had an average 2007 per capita income of $32,443, more than eight times the average for the least free countries. Similarly the average annual growth rate of the top group was 2.4 percent, compared to 0.9 percent for the bottom group.

When low-income countries get the institutions and policies right, they are able to achieve exceedingly high growth rates and narrow the income gap relative to high-income industrial nations. Countries and jurisdictions like Hong Kong, Singapore, Taiwan, Ireland, Chile, Mauritius, and

Botswana illustrate this point. During recent decades, all of these have made substantial moves toward economic freedom, and all of them have grown rapidly and achieved substantial increases in income levels and living standards. In 1980 the two most populous countries, China and India, were also among the world's least free economies. During the 1980s and 1990s, they adopted policies more consistent with economic freedom, and they, too, are now achieving impressive rates of economic growth.

Since the mid-1980s, many less developed countries have moved substantially toward economic freedom. The countries moving the most toward economic freedom have grown more rapidly. This has been a major contributing factor to the sharp decline in the world's poverty rate. The World Bank classifies a person as living in "extreme poverty" if their income is less than $1.25 per day. In 2005, the world's extreme poverty rate was 25 percent, down from 58 percent in 1980. Thus, the extreme poverty rate is now less than half the figure of a quarter century ago. Persons with incomes of less than $2 per day are classified as living in moderate poverty. The world's moderate poverty rate fell from 75 percent in 1980 to 46 percent in 2005. Less developed countries with the highest economic freedom ratings and/or the largest increases in economic freedom achieved the largest reductions in poverty during this period.[25]

Both economic theory and the empirical evidence indicate that countries attract more investment, grow more rapidly, and achieve higher income levels when they adopt and maintain policies along the lines outlined in this section. The key to economic progress is to get the institutions and policies right. The sooner political and opinion leaders throughout the world begin moving their countries toward greater economic freedom, the more prosperous the world will be.

PART III

Economic Progress and the
Role of Government

TEN ELEMENTS OF CLEAR THINKING ABOUT ECONOMIC PROGRESS AND THE ROLE OF GOVERNMENT

1. Government promotes economic progress by protecting the rights of individuals and supplying a few goods that are difficult to provide through markets.

2. Allocation through political voting is fundamentally different from market allocation, and economic analysis indicates that the latter is more consistent with economic progress.

3. The costs of government are not only taxes.

4. Unless restrained by constitutional rules, special-interest groups will use the democratic political process to fleece taxpayers and consumers.

5. Unless restrained by constitutional rules, legislators will run budget deficits and spend excessively.

6. Government slows economic progress when it becomes heavily involved in providing favors to some at the expense of others.

7. The net gain to those receiving government transfers is less, and often substantially less, than the amount they receive.

8. Central planning replaces markets with politics, which wastes resources and retards economic progress.

9. Competition is just as important in government as in markets.

10. Constitutional rules that bring the political process and sound economics into harmony will promote economic progress.

Introduction

Government is a little bit like food. Food is essential, but when consumed excessively, it leads to obesity, energy loss, and other health-related problems. Similarly, when constrained within proper boundaries, government can be a powerful force for prosperity. But when it expands excessively and undertakes activities for which it is ill-suited, it undermines economic progress.

When decisions are made democratically, it is particularly important for voters to understand the economics of political action. All too often, policies are evaluated on the basis of the stated objectives of their proponents rather than their likely effectiveness. Put another way, good intentions often triumph over sound policies. Moreover, potentially adverse secondary effects are often ignored. As a result, expectations are unrealistic and disappointment soon follows.

Economics provides considerable insight on the operation of the political process. This section uses the tools of economics to analyze how the democratic political process works. We will consider both the conditions that strengthen the case for government action and those that weaken it. We will explain why political results often differ substantially from those that are promised. We will also explain why there is a built-in tendency for governments to expand and undertake activities that waste resources and reduce the income levels of the citizenry. Finally, we will outline a set of constitutional rules that would direct government action more consistently toward activities that enhance the quality of our lives.

1. Government Promotes Economic Progress by Protecting the Rights of Individuals and Supplying a Few Goods That Are Difficult to Provide Through Markets.

A wise and frugal government, which shall restrain men from injuring one another, which shall leave them otherwise free to regulate their own pursuits of industry and improvements, and shall not take from the mouth of labor the bread it has earned. This is the sum of good government.[1]

—THOMAS JEFFERSON

A government can promote social cooperation and enhance its citizens' economic welfare primarily in two ways: (1) by providing people with protection for their lives, liberties, and properties (as long as the properties and liberties were acquired without force, fraud, or theft) and (2) by supplying a few select goods that have unusual characteristics that make them difficult to provide through markets. Nobel laureate James Buchanan refers to these functions, respectively, as the protective and productive functions of government.

The protective function encompasses the government's maintenance of a framework of security and order, including the enforcement of rules against theft, fraud, and violence. Government has a monopoly on the legitimate use of force in order to protect citizens from one another and from outsiders. Thus the protective state seeks to prevent individuals from harming one another and to maintain an infrastructure of rules that allow people to interact with one another harmoniously. The crucial ingredients of this infrastructure include the protection of people and their property against aggressors; unbiased enforcement of contracts; equal treatment under the law; and avoidance of discriminatory regulations, taxes, and subsidies.

When government performs its protective function well, individuals can have confidence that they will not be cheated and that the wealth they create will not be taken from them—by either selfish intruders or the government itself through high taxes and excessive regulations or the ravages of inflation. This protection provides citizens with assurance that if they sow, they will be permitted to reap. When this is true, people will sow and reap abundantly, and economic progress will result.

Problems arise when a government performs its protective function poorly. If private ownership rights are not clearly defined and enforced, some parties will engage in harmful actions toward others. They will take property that does not belong to them and use resources without paying for them. When people are allowed to impose such costs on others without just compensation, markets do not accurately register the true cost of producing goods. So when property rights to resources are poorly defined and enforced, the resources tend to be overused and underprotected.

The second primary function of government, the productive function, involves the provision of what economists call public goods. Such goods have two distinguishing characteristics: (1) supplying them to one individual simultaneously makes them available to others, and (2) it is difficult, if not impossible, to restrict their consumption to paying customers only. A few goods—national defense, flood-control projects, and mosquito-abatement programs provide examples—have these public good characteristics.

It is difficult for private businesses to produce and market public goods. The nature of a public good makes it impossible for a private business to establish a one-to-one link between payment and receipt of the goods. This gives the customer little incentive to buy the goods or services. After all, if others buy the goods, you can consume them without paying for them. If a firm builds a dam to control flooding, for example, it will be difficult, if not impossible, to provide the flood control only to paying customers and to withhold it from those who don't pay. Recognizing this difficulty, the potential beneficiaries are generally unwilling to help cover the cost of the project. Everybody has an incentive to let "the other person" pay. When this happens, however, the project may not be undertaken even though it is worth more than its cost.

In most cases it is easy to establish a link between payment and receipt. If you do not pay for a gallon of ice cream, an automobile, television set, smart phone, MP3 player, and literally thousands of other items, suppliers will not provide them to you and you cannot freely benefit from those items purchased by others. Thus, there are very few public goods and services. But when the nature of these public products makes it difficult to link payment and receipt, citizens may be able to gain from government action. In essence, government provision of public goods is what Abraham Lincoln had in mind when he stated: "The legitimate object of government is to do for a community of people whatever they need to have done, but cannot do, *at all,* or cannot, *so well do,* in their separate and individual capacities."[2]

Americans have had an on-again, off-again love affair with government. The U.S. Constitution enumerated limited functions for the federal government and, for more than a century, kept the government pretty much within the protective and productive boundaries outlined here. Even though the Great Depression was largely the result of mismanagement (for example, a sharp reduction in the money supply, a huge increase in tariffs in 1930, and a large tax increase in 1932), government greatly expanded its role in the economy. By the 1960s many Americans believed government could do almost anything. Income transfers were going to greatly reduce, if not eliminate, poverty. Medicare and Medicaid would mean "free" health care for the elderly and the poor. And budget deficits were going to stimulate economic activity and reduce the rate of unemployment. From the Great Depression forward, government moved well beyond its protective and productive functions. On careful examination, the results were far less impressive than the promises.

By 1980 the ineffectiveness and adverse side effects of the expanded role of government were evident, and cooled the people's love affair with government. Consequently, government pulled back on many levels. Reductions in the relative size of government occurred for almost two decades and a balanced budget was achieved for a brief period. As expected, economic progress resulted. Under the administration of George W. Bush, this changed. Government once again expanded, its spending soared, and it became more involved in private market affairs. Government subsidies and loose lending regulations, coupled with expansionary monetary policy, induced many to expand and use their lines of credit and purchase things that they could not afford, including high-priced homes. In essence, the regulatory erosion of mortgage lending standards and credit expansion fueled the housing boom. But these actions also generated the conditions that led to the economic bust—excessive debt, rising default rates, and the financial crisis. Nonetheless, the government's response to the crisis was further expansion in the size and role of government—even though its policies were the fundamental cause of the crisis! This was a repeat of what happened during the Great Depression.

Economics helps one better understand how the political process works. It replaces naive romanticism with realistic expectations. The latter may not be as much fun, but achieving a solid understanding of government and its incentive structure in a democracy will enhance our knowledge of both its potential and its limitations as a tool for economic progress.

2. Allocation Through Political Voting Is Fundamentally Different from Market Allocation, and Economic Analysis Indicates That the Latter Is More Consistent with Economic Progress.

There is a tendency to idealize the democratic political process. Some act as if a policy favored by the majority is automatically sound. It is important to distinguish between the use of voting (1) to elect representatives who will carry out the functions of government and (2) to plan, direct, and control the economy. The case for the former is impeccable, but the case for the latter is weak at best.

The political process is merely an alternative form of social organization. It is not a corrective device that can be counted on to provide a sound remedy when problems arise. Even when it is controlled by elected political officials, there is no assurance that government actions will be productive. This is particularly true when governments become heavily involved in allocating scarce resources toward favored sectors, businesses, and interest groups.

Clearly, policies favored by a majority do not always make us better off. Consider a simple economy with five voters. Suppose three of the voters favor a project that gives them net benefits of $2 each, but imposes net cost of $5 each on the other two voters. In aggregate, the project generates net costs of $10 against net benefits of only $6. It is counterproductive and will make the five-person society worse off. Nonetheless, if decided by majority vote, it will pass three to two. Increasing the number of voters from 5 to 5 million or 200 million will not alter the general point. Neither will a proportional expansion in the net benefits and costs. As this simple example illustrates, majority voting can clearly lead to the adoption of counterproductive projects.

It is useful to compare democratic political allocation with markets, the major alternative form of economic organization. It is particularly important to keep the following three points in mind.

First, majority rule provides the basis for government action, while market activity is based on mutual agreement and voluntary exchange. In a democratic setting, when a majority, either directly or through their elected representatives, adopts a policy, the minority is forced to pay for its support even if they strongly disagree. For example, if the majority votes for a new baseball stadium, a housing subsidy program, or the bailout of an automobile company, minority voters are forced to yield and pay taxes for support of such projects even if they are harmed. The power to tax and regulate makes it possible for the majority to coerce the minority. There is no such parallel coercive power when resources are allocated by markets. Market exchanges do not occur unless all parties agree. Private firms can charge a high price, but they cannot force anyone to buy. Indeed, operating without government assistance, private firms must provide consumers with benefits that exceed the price charged in order to attract customers.

Second, there is little incentive for voters to be well informed about either candidates or issues. In a large number setting, an individual voter will not decide the outcome of an election. The typical voter is more likely to be struck by lightning on the way to the polling place than that his or her vote will be decisive in a statewide election. Recognizing this point, most voters spend little, if any, time and energy studying issues and candidates in order to cast a well-informed vote. Most simply decide on the basis of information acquired as the result of their other activities (watching television, interactions with friends, or discussions at the office). Given these incentives, it is not surprising that most voters have no idea where candidates stand or what impact government actions (ranging from agricultural subsidies to trade restrictions) have on the economy. Economists refer to this as the rational ignorance effect.

The weak incentive of voters to make informed choices is in sharp contrast to that of consumers in private markets. Market consumers individually decide how to spend their money, and if they make bad choices, they personally bear the consequences. This incentive structure provides them with motivation to both make informed choices and spend their money wisely. Thus, when consumers consider the purchase of an automobile, an apartment, a personal computer, a gym membership, or one of thousands of similar items, they have a strong incentive to make well-informed choices.

Third, the political process imposes the same option on everyone, while markets allow for diverse representation. Put another way, government allocation results in a "one size fits all" outcome, while markets allow different individuals and groups to vote for and receive desired options. For example, when schooling is allocated through the market rather than supplied by the government, some parents choose schools that stress religious values, while others opt for secularism; still others select schools that emphasize basic skills, cultural diversity, or vocational preparation. Individual buyers (or members of a group) willing to pay the cost are able to choose a desired educational option and receive it. Markets provide for a system of proportional representation, which makes it possible for more people to obtain goods and services more consistent with their preferences. Moreover, it also avoids conflicts that inevitably arise when the majority imposes its will on various minorities.

It is informative to compare and contrast markets and government with regard to the incentive of decision makers to undertake productive projects and refrain from counterproductive ones. As we learned earlier, consumers who value a good or service enough to pay more than the cost of the resources required for its production, enable firms to earn profits by serving them. In contrast, if consumers do not value a product enough to pay a price that will cover its costs, losses will discipline firms that misallocate resources. Thus, the profit-and-loss mechanism of a market economy tends to direct resources toward productive projects and away from those that are unproductive.

Even when it is controlled through voting, the political process does not have anything like profits and losses that can be counted on to direct resources toward productive and away from counterproductive activities. Instead, when unconstrained by constitutional limits, elected officials gain votes by taking resources from some and using them to "buy" the votes of a majority. As the saying goes, if you take from Peter and give to Paul, you can usually count on the support of Paul.

To a large degree, the modern political process is about various coalitions trading contributions, high-paying jobs, and other forms of support to political officials in exchange for subsidies, spending programs, and regulations that provide well-organized groups with favors at the expense of others. As this happens, more resources move toward lobbying and other favor-seeking activities and fewer toward production and development of more and better products. Taxes will rise and businesses (and other organizations) with effective favor-seeking programs will expand relative to those producing goods and services that are highly valued relative to cost. Predictably, this incentive structure reduces the productive use of resources, expands counterproductive activities, and keeps income levels well below their potential.

The framers of the U.S. Constitution were aware that even a democratic government might undertake counterproductive actions. Thus, they incorporated restraints on the economic role of government. They enumerated the permissible tax and spending powers of the central government (Article I, Section 8) and allocated all other powers to the states and the people (Tenth Amendment). They also prohibited states from adopting legislation "impairing the obligation of contracts" (Article I, Section 10). Furthermore, the Fifth Amendment specifies that private property shall not be "taken for public use without just compensation." Over time, however, Supreme Court decisions eroded these restraints and government control over both individuals and businesses expanded, as did federal control over the states. As we proceed, we will analyze in more detail the operation of the democratic political process and consider modifications that might bring it more into harmony with economic growth and prosperity.

3. The Costs of Government Are Not Only Taxes.

Politicians often speak as if taxes measure the cost of government. While taxes impose a cost, they are only part of the cost, and in some cases only a small part, of actions undertaken by the government. The cost of any product is what we have to give up in order to produce it, and government is no exception. There are three types of costs incurred when governments levy taxes and provide goods and services.

First, there is the loss of private-sector output that could have been produced with the resources that are now employed producing the goods and services supplied by the government. The resources that go into police protection, highways, missiles, education, health care, or any other "government project" have alternative uses. If they were not tied up producing goods and services supplied through the public sector, they would be available to the private sector. This cost is incurred regardless of whether public-sector goods are paid for by current taxes, an increase in government debt, or money creation. It can be diminished only by reducing the size of government purchases.

The second type of cost is the cost of resources expended in the collection of taxes and the enforcement of, and compliance with, government mandates. Tax laws and regulatory orders must be enforced. Tax returns and formal notices of compliance with regulations must be prepared and monitored. In the United States, studies indicate that it takes businesses and individuals approximately 5.5 billion worker hours (the hours worked by 2.7 million full-time workers) each year just to complete the taxation paperwork. In 2004, the cost of enforcement and compliance with tax laws and regulatory mandates was estimated to be $1.1 trillion dollars. This is approximately $8,500 per household, or 11 percent of national income.[3] These costs do not appear in federal expenditures, nor in tax collections, but nonetheless represent the forced expenditures by private firms to meet the regulatory requirement of the federal government.

Third, there is the cost of price distortions resulting from taxes and borrowing. Taxes distort incentives. They drive a wedge between what buyers pay and sellers receive. (With taxes, buyers pay more, but sellers receive less than what the buyer pays.) Some otherwise mutually advantageous exchanges will become unprofitable and therefore not occur. Giving up these potential gains imposes a cost on the economy. In other cases, taxes may induce individuals to allocate more time to leisure or nonmarket activities, which also reduces output. Some people will engage in tax-avoidance activities, which will impose an additional cost on the economy. Research indicates that these deadweight losses add between 9 and 16 percent to the cost of taxation, over and above the costs of enforcement and compliance. These costs should be considered when analyzing the merits of government programs.

It is also important to recognize that politicians have an incentive to conceal the cost of government. As former Senate Majority Leader Robert Dole noted when quoting Jean-Baptiste Colbert, French economist and minister of finance under King Louis XIV: "Taxing is much like plucking a goose. It is the art of getting the greatest number of feathers with the least amount of hissing."[4] The political attractiveness of budget deficits, money creation, and various indirect taxes stems from the desire of politicians to conceal the costs of government programs.

Deception about business taxes is particularly widespread. Politicians often speak of imposing taxes on "business" as if part of the tax burden could be transferred from individuals to a nonperson (business). Purely and simply, business taxes, like all other taxes, are paid by individuals. A corporation or business firm may write the check to the government, but it does not pay the taxes. The business firm merely collects the money from someone else—its customers, employees, or stockholders—and transfers what is collected to the government. It may be good political rhetoric to talk about "business" taxes, but the fact is that taxes, and all other costs of government, are paid for by people.

4. Unless Restrained by Constitutional Rules, Special-Interest Groups Will Use the Democratic Political Process to Fleece Taxpayers and Consumers.

When public policy is limited to its proper functions, government can contribute mightily to economic prosperity. However, this requires more than majority rule and the popular election of legislators.

Unfortunately, democratically elected officials can often benefit by supporting policies that favor special-interest groups at the expense of the general public. Consider a policy that generates substantial personal gain for the members of a well-organized group (for example, an association representing business interests, members of a labor union, or a farm group) at the expense of the broader interests of taxpayers or consumers. While the organized interest group has fewer members than the total number of taxpayers or consumers, *individually* their personal gain from the legislation is likely to be large. In contrast, while many taxpayers and consumers are harmed, the cost imposed on each is small, and the source of the cost is often difficult to identify.

For issues of this kind, it is easy to see why politicians often support special-interest groups. Since the personal stake of the interest group members is substantial, they have a powerful incentive to form alliances and let candidates and legislators know how strongly they feel about the issue. Many interest group members will decide who to vote for and who to support financially almost exclusively on the basis of a politician's stand on issues of special importance to them. In contrast, as the rational ignorance effect indicates, the bulk of voters will be generally uninformed and they will not care much about the special-interest issue because it exerts little impact on their personal welfare.

If you were a vote-seeking politician, what would you do? Clearly you would not get much campaign support by favoring the interests of the largely uninformed and uninterested majority. But you can get vocal supporters, campaign workers, and most important, campaign contributions by favoring the special-interest issue. In the age of media politics, politicians are under strong pressure to support special interests, tap them for campaign funds, and use the contributions to project a positive candidate image on television and the Internet. Politicians unwilling to play this game—those unwilling to use the government treasury to provide well-organized interest groups with favors in exchange for political support—are seriously disadvantaged. Given the incentive structure, politicians are led as if by an invisible hand to reflect the views of special-interest groups, even though this often leads to policies that, summed across all voters, will be seriously wasteful.

The power of special interests is further strengthened by logrolling and pork-barrel legislation. Logrolling involves the practice of politicians trading votes to get the necessary support to pass desired legislation. Pork-barrel legislation is the term used to describe the bundling of unrelated projects benefiting many interests into a single bill. Both logrolling and pork-barrel legislation will often make it possible for counterproductive projects benefiting concentrated interests to gain legislative approval.

Exhibit 7 illustrates how pork-barrel politics and vote trading reinforce the special-interest effect and lead to the adoption of counterproductive projects. In this simple example, a five-member legislature is considering three projects: (1) a bridge to nowhere in District A, (2) construction of an indoor rain forest in District B, and (3) subsidies for ethanol that generates benefits for the corn farmers of District C. For each district,

Exhibit 7: Trading Votes and Passing
Counterproductive Legislation

		NET BENEFITS (+) OR COSTS (−) TO VOTERS IN EQUAL SIZE DISTRICTS		
Voters of District	Bridge to Nowhere	Indoor Rainforest Project	Ethanol Subsidy	Total
A	$100	−$30	−$30	$40
B	−$30	$100	−$30	$40
C	−$30	−$30	$100	$40
D	−$30	−$30	−$30	−$90
E	−$30	−$30	−$30	−$90
Total	**−$20**	**−$20**	**−$20**	**−$60**

the net benefit or cost is shown—that is, the benefit to the district minus the tax cost imposed on it. The total cost of each of the three projects exceeds the benefits (as shown by the negative number in the total row at the bottom of the table), and therefore each is counterproductive. If the projects were voted on separately, each would lose by a 4-to-1 vote because only one district would gain, and the other four would lose. However, when the projects are bundled together through either logrolling (representatives A, B, and C could agree to trade votes) or pork-barrel legislation (all three programs put on the same bill), they can all pass, despite the fact that all are inefficient. This can be seen by noting that the total combined net benefit is positive for representatives A, B, and C. Given the weak incentive for voters to acquire information, those harmed by pork-barreling and other special-interest policies are unlikely to even be aware of them. Thus, the incentive to support special-interest projects, including those that are counterproductive, is even stronger than is implied by the simple numeric example of Exhibit 7.

The bottom line is clear: Representative government based solely on majority rule does not handle special-interest issues well. The tendency of the unrestrained political process to favor well-organized groups helps explain the presence of many programs that reduce the size of the economic pie. For example, consider the case of the roughly sixty thousand sugar beet and cane growers in the United States. For many years, the price of sugar paid by American consumers has been two or three times the world sugar price because of the highly restrictive quotas imposed by the federal government. As a result of this program, sugar growers gain about $1.9 billion, more than $30,000 per grower on average. Most of these benefits are reaped by large growers whose owners have incomes far above the national average. On the other hand, these subsidies cost the average American household about $20 per year in the form of higher prices for products containing sugar. Even more important, the resources of Americans are wasted producing a good we are ill suited to produce and one that could be obtained at a substantially lower cost through trade. As a result Americans are worse off.

Nonetheless, Congress continues to support the program, and it is easy to see why. Given the sizable impact on their personal wealth, it is perfectly sensible for sugar growers, particularly the large ones, to use their wealth and political clout to help politicians who support their interests. This is precisely what they do. During the two most recent election cycles, the sugar lobby contributed more than $16 million to candidates and political action committees. In contrast, it makes no sense for the average voter to investigate this issue or give it any significant weight when deciding how he or she is going to vote. In fact, most voters are unaware that this program costs them money. As a result, politicians can gain by continuing to support the sugar growers even though the subsidy program wastes resources and reduces the wealth of the nation.[5]

The fleecing of taxpayers and consumers in order to provide benefits to identifiable and politically active voting blocs has become the primary business of modern politics. Taxpayers and consumers spend approximately $20 billion annually to support grain, cotton, tobacco, peanut, wool, and dairy programs, all of which have the same structure as the sugar program. The political power of special interests also explains the presence of tariffs and quotas on steel, shoes, brooms, textiles, and many other products. Federally funded irrigation projects, subsidies to General Motors, and support programs for other large businesses, airports and sports stadiums in specific districts as well as ethanol producers (the list goes on and on) are all policies politically motivated by special-interest effects rather than the net benefits to Americans. While each such program individually imposes only a small drag on our economy, together they bust the federal budget, waste resources, and significantly lower our standard of living.

The framers of the U.S. Constitution were aware of this defect of democratic politics. (They called the interest groups "factions.") The Constitution sought to limit pressure from the factions in Article I, Section 8, which specifies that Congress is to levy only *uniform* taxes for programs that promote the *common* defense and *general* welfare. This clause was designed to preclude the use of general tax revenue to provide benefits to subgroups of the population. However, through the years court decisions and legislative acts have gutted and distorted its meaning. Thus, as it is currently interpreted, the Constitution now fails to constrain the political power of well-organized special-interest groups.

5. Unless Restrained by Constitutional Rules, Legislators Will Run Budget Deficits and Spend Excessively.

The attractiveness of financing spending by debt issue to the elected politicians should be obvious. Borrowing allows spending to be made that will yield immediate political payoffs without the incurring of any immediate political cost.[6]

—James Buchanan

When a government's spending exceeds its revenues, a budget deficit results. Governments generally issue interest-earning bonds to finance their budget deficits. These bonds issued by the U.S. Treasury comprise the national debt. A budget deficit increases the size of the national debt by the amount of the deficit. In contrast, a budget surplus allows the federal government to pay off bondholders and thereby reduce the size of its outstanding debt. Basically the national debt represents the cumulative effect of all the prior budget deficits and surpluses.

Prior to 1960 almost everyone—including the leading figures of both political parties—thought that the government should balance its budget except perhaps during times of war. There was widespread implicit agreement—much like a constitutional rule—that the federal budget should be balanced. Given these political pressures, the budget of the federal government was generally near balance during peacetime. Except during times of war, both deficits and surpluses were small relative to the size of the economy.

The Keynesian revolution changed all of this. Keynesians—those accepting the views of English economist John Maynard Keynes—believed that changes in government spending and budget deficits could help promote a more stable economy. They argued that, rather than balancing the budget, the government should run a budget deficit during periods of recession and shift toward a budget surplus when there was concern about inflation. In short, the Keynesian revolution released political decision makers from the discipline imposed by a balanced budget. Freed from this constraint, politicians consistently spent more than they were willing to tax.

Exhibit 8 shows the path of the federal deficit measured as a share of GDP since 1960. While the deficits have been larger during recessions, perpetual deficits have been the norm during the past 50 years. The federal deficit averaged about 2 percent of GDP between 1960 and 1980 and

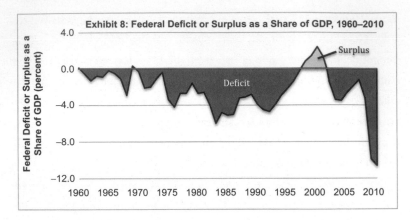

Source: Office of Management and Budget, *President's Budget *FY 2011 Budget, Table 1.3.*
http://www.whitehouse.gov/omb/budget/historicals/

the figure was even larger during the 1980s. The deficits were smaller during the 1990s and surpluses were even achieved from 1998 to 2000. But the era of deficit control was exceedingly short. The surpluses quickly evaporated and deficits have once again soared to new highs, reaching 10 percent of GDP during the recession of 2009–2010.

Of course, large deficits push the national debt upward. Measured as a share of GDP, the outstanding federal debt has risen from 58 percent in 2000 to 70 percent in 2008, and 98 percent in 2010. The federal debt now stands at the highest level since the period immediately following World War II.

The political attractiveness of spending financed by borrowing rather than taxation is not surprising. It reflects what economists call the short-sightedness effect: the tendency of elected political officials to favor projects that generate immediate, highly visible benefits at the expense of costs that can be cast into the future and are difficult to identify. Legislators have a strong incentive to spend money on programs that benefit the voters in their district and special-interest groups that will help them win reelection. They do not like to tax, since taxes impose a visible cost on voters. Debt is an alternative to current taxes; it pushes the *visible* cost of government into the future. Budget deficits and borrowing allow politicians to supply voters with immediate benefits without having to impose a parallel visible cost in the form of higher taxes. Thus, deficits are a natural outgrowth of unrestrained democratic politics.

The unconstrained political process plays into the hands of well-organized interest groups and encourages government spending to gain rich patronage benefits for a few at the expense of many. Each representative has a strong incentive to fight hard for expenditures beneficial to his or her constituents and has little incentive to oppose spending by others. In contrast, there is little incentive for a legislator to be a spending "watchdog." A legislative watchdog would incur the wrath of colleagues who find it more difficult to deliver special programs for their districts and retaliate by providing little support for spending in the watchdog's district. More important, the benefits of spending cuts and deficit reductions that the watchdog is trying to attain (for example, lower taxes and lower interest rates) will be spread so thinly among all voters that the legislator's constituents will reap only a small part of these benefits.

Perhaps the following illustration will help explain why it is so difficult for the 435 representatives and 100 senators to bring federal spending and the budget deficit under control. Suppose these 535 individuals go out to dinner knowing that after the meal each will receive a bill for 1/535th of the cost. No one feels compelled to order less because his or her restraint will exert little impact on the total bill. Why not order shrimp for an appetizer, entrees of steak and lobster, and a large piece of cheesecake for dessert? After all, the extra spending will add only a few pennies to each person's share of the total bill. For example, if one member of the dinner party orders expensive items that push up the total bill by $10, his share of the cost will be less than 2 cents. What a bargain! Of course, he will have to pay extra for the extravagant orders of the other 534 diners. But that's true no matter what he orders. The result is that everyone ends up ordering extravagantly and paying more for extras that provide little value relative to cost.[7]

The federal government financed approximately 40 percent of its expenditures by borrowing during both 2009 and 2010. This increased the federal debt by nearly $3 trillion in just two years. These huge deficits have pushed the federal debt to dangerously high levels. Moreover, the future benefits promised to senior citizens under the Social Security and Medicare programs are far greater than the payroll tax revenues that provide their financing. These unfunded liabilities are another form of debt. In fact, the debt implied by the unfunded Social Security and Medicare liabilities is almost four times the size of the official national debt. As the baby boomers move into the retirement phase of life in the years immediately ahead, spending on Social Security and Medicare will outstrip the revenues for their finance, further complicating the debt liability of the federal government.

What will happen if the federal government does not bring its finances under control? As a nation's debt gets larger and larger relative to the size of the economy, there will be repercussions in credit markets. Extension of loans to the government of a country with a large debt/GDP ratio is risky. As a result, the highly indebted government will have to pay higher interest rates. In turn, the higher interest costs will make it even more difficult to control spending and keep taxes at reasonable levels. If the debt continues to rise relative to income, investors will become more and more reluctant to buy the bonds issued by the U.S. Treasury. Eventually it will lead to a financial crisis—either outright default by the government or finance of the debt by money creation and inflation. In either case, there will be a destructive impact on the economy. This has occurred in other countries that have failed to control government finances and the U.S. is not immune to the laws of economics.

It is vitally important for the federal government to control its spending and borrowing in the years ahead. This is unlikely to happen without a change in the political rules. The rules need to be changed so it will be more difficult for politicians to spend more than they are willing to tax. There are several ways this might be done. The Constitution might be amended to require the federal government to balance its budget, even as most state governments are required to do. Or a constitutional amendment could require two-thirds or three-fourths approval by both Houses of Congress for spending proposals and increases in the federal government's borrowing power. Or this year's spending might be limited to last year's level of revenues. Proposed rule changes of this kind would make it more difficult for legislators to spend unless they were willing to tax or to charge users for the government services.

Such rule changes would stiffen the government's budget constraint and force legislators to consider more carefully the costs of government programs. An improvement in the cost-effectiveness of government would result.

6. Government Slows Economic Progress When It Becomes Heavily Involved in Providing Favors to Some at the Expense of Others.

The tool of politics (which frequently becomes its objective) is to extract resources from the general taxpayer with minimum offense and to distribute the proceeds among innumerable claimants in such a way to maximize the support at the polls. Politics, so far as mobilizing support is concerned, represents the art of calculated cheating or, more precisely, how to cheat without being really caught.[8]

—JAMES R. SCHLESINGER, FORMER SECRETARY OF DEFENSE

There are two ways individuals can acquire wealth: production and plunder. People can get ahead by producing goods or services of value and exchanging them for income. This method of acquiring income helps the exchanging partners and enhances the wealth of society. But sometimes the rules also allow people to get ahead by "plundering" what others have produced. That is, the gain of one is a loss to another. This method not only fails to generate additional income but also consumes resources and thereby reduces the wealth of the society.

Governments promote economic prosperity when they encourage productive activity and discourage plunder. A government that acts as a neutral force, protecting property rights and enforcing contracts, can best achieve this objective. When the effective law of the land makes it difficult to take the property of others, few resources will flow into plunder. Moreover, in that ideal situation the resources employed defending against actions of plunder will also be small.

In the modern world, government can be, and often is, used as an agent for plunder. The quantity of scarce resources directed toward lobbying, political campaigns, and the various forms of "favor seeking" from the government will be directly proportional to the ease with which the political process can be used for personal (or interest group) gain at the expense of others. When a government fails to allocate the cost of public-sector projects to the primary beneficiaries (through user fees, for example), or when it becomes heavily involved in income-transfer activities, people will spend more time organizing and lobbying politicians and less time producing goods and services.[9] Resources that would otherwise be used to create wealth and generate income are wasted fighting over slices of an economic pie that is smaller than it could be. Note: Economists refer to these lobbying and other favor-seeking activities as rent seeking.

Transfers and subsidies now account for approximately half of the federal budget. Social Security and healthcare subsidies comprise the bulk of the spending, but there were more than 2,000 federal subsidy programs in

2010, up from 1,425 just a decade earlier.[10] Numerous activities are subsidized, including irrigation of arid lands, ethanol-enriched gasoline, mortgage housing loans, export of aircraft, small business start-ups, hiring of persons unemployed more than six weeks, solar panels, construction of low-cost housing, research on global warming, loans to college students, and production of agricultural goods ranging from corn and cotton to peanuts and wheat, just to list a few. The subsidies distort prices, favor some producers and consumers relative to others, plunder the taxpayer, and undermine the operation of markets. Business after business is spending more time and resources searching for subsidies in Washington and less time and resources developing better and more economical products.

Control of subsidies, as well as more general government spending, is complicated by the fact that nearly half of all Americans pay no personal income tax. Moreover, this share has been increasing. These nontaxpayers have little reason to resist increases in government spending because they do not expect to pay for them. In fact, they have every incentive to pressure politicians for more government services and transfers because those who actually pay taxes will have to pick up the tab.

The growth of transfers and subsidies is undermining both the political process and operation of markets. Increasingly, government is about taking from taxpayers and using the revenues to favor specified voting blocs in exchange for political contributions and support. In a statement widely attributed to Scotsman Alexander Tytler, he argues that "A democracy cannot exist as a permanent form of government. It can only exist until the voters discover that they can vote themselves largesse from the public treasury. From that moment on, the majority always votes for the candidates promising the most benefits from the public treasury, with the result that a democracy always collapses over loose fiscal policy."[11]

Counterproductive, favor-seeking activities are an outgrowth of unrestrained democracy. As the transfers grow and government spending increases, democratic politics resembles a cafeteria food fight. High taxes undermine productive incentives; lobbying, corruption and other counterproductive activities grow; and the economy stagnates while the budget deficit soars. Unless the constitutional protection of property rights and limitations on the spending, subsidizing, and borrowing activities of government are restored, democratically elected politicians will continue to enact programs that waste resources and impair the general standard of living. Eventually this path will lead to a collapse of government credit or inflation, or both.

7. The Net Gain to Those Receiving Government Transfers Is Less, and Often Substantially Less, Than the Amount They Receive.

When the War on Poverty was declared in the mid-1960s, President Lyndon Johnson and other proponents of the program argued that poverty could be eliminated if only Americans were willing to transfer a little more income to the less fortunate members of society. They were willing (or at least their political representatives were), and income-transfer programs expanded substantially. Measured as *a proportion of total income,* transfers directed toward the poor (for example, Aid to Families with Dependent Children, food stamps, and Medicaid) doubled during the 1965–75 period. Since 1975, income transfers have continued to grow as a share of national income.

Remember, good intentions do not guarantee a desired outcome, and the War on Poverty spending provides yet another illustration of this point. As Exhibit 9 shows, the poverty rate was declining rapidly prior to the War on Poverty. It fell from 32 percent in 1947 to 13.9 percent in 1965. The downward trend continued for a few more years, reaching 10 percent in 1968. In the late 1960s, only a few years after the War on Poverty transfers were initiated, improvement came to a halt. The poverty rate began to level off rather than continue its decline. Since 1970 it has fluctuated within a narrow band around the 10 percent level. In 2005 the

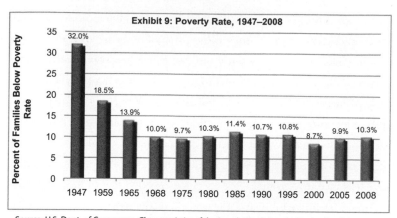

Source: U.S. Dept. of Commerce, *Characteristics of the Population Below the Poverty Level: 1982, Table 5*; and U.S. Census Bureau, Historical Poverty Tables—Families. http://www.census.gov/hhes/www/poverty/histpov/hstpov4.xls.

poverty rate was 9.9 percent and it stood at 10.3 percent in 2008, almost exactly the level achieved four decades earlier. Given that income per person, adjusted for inflation, has more than doubled since the late 1960s, this lack of progress is startling.

Why weren't the income transfers more effective? Economic analysis indicates that their ineffectiveness reflects a general proposition: It is difficult to transfer income to a group of recipients in a manner that will improve their long-term well-being. Once again, this proposition reflects the *unintended consequences of secondary effects.*[12]

Three major factors undermine the effectiveness of income transfers, regardless of whom they are directed toward.

First, an increase in government transfers will reduce the incentive of both the taxpayer-donor and the transfer recipient to earn income. Economic growth will thereby be retarded. Income is not like manna from heaven. Neither is national income an economic pie that is baked by the government so slices of various sizes can be served up hot to people throughout the country. On the contrary, income is something that people produce and earn. Individuals earn income as they provide goods and services to others willing to pay for them. We can think of national income as an economic pie, but it is a pie whose size is determined by the actions of millions of people, each using production and trade to earn an individual slice. It is impossible to redistribute portions of the slices they earn without simultaneously reducing their work effort and innovative actions that generate the income.

As taxes are increased to finance a higher level of transfers, taxpayers have less incentive to make the sacrifices needed to produce and earn, and more incentive to invest in wasteful tax shelters to try to hang on to the cash they've earned. Similarly, since benefits decline as the recipient's income increases, the transfer recipient will also have less incentive to earn because additional earnings will increase net income by only a fraction—and in many cases only a small fraction—of the additional earnings. Thus neither taxpayers nor transfer recipients will produce and earn as much as they would in the absence of the transfer program.

To see the negative effect of almost any transfer policy on productive effort, consider the reaction of students if a professor announces at the beginning of the term that the grading policy for the class will redistribute the points earned on the exams so that no one will receive less than a C. Under this plan, students who earned A grades by scoring an average of 90 percent or higher on the exams would have to give up enough of their points to bring up the average of those who would otherwise get Ds and Fs. And of course the B students would also have to contribute some of their points as well, although not as many, in order to achieve a more equal grade distribution.

Does anyone doubt that the students who would have made As and Bs will study less hard when their extra effort is "taxed" to provide benefits to others? And so would the students who would have made Cs and Ds, since the penalty they paid for less effort would be cushioned by point transfers they would lose if they earned more points on their own.

The same logic applies even to those who would have made Fs, although they probably weren't doing very much studying anyway. Predictably, the outcome will be less studying, and overall achievement will decline. The impact of tax-transfer schemes will be similar: less work effort and lower overall income levels.

Second, competition for transfers will erode most of the long-term gain of the intended beneficiaries. Governments must establish a criterion for the receipt of income transfers and other political favors. If it did not do so, the transfers would bust the budget. Generally, the government will require a transfer recipient to own something, do something, or be something. However, once the criterion is established, people will modify their behavior to qualify for the "free" money or other government favors. As they do so, their net gain from the transfers declines.

Think about the following: Suppose that the U.S. government decided to give away a $50 bill between 9:00 a.m. and 5:00 p.m. each weekday to all persons willing to wait in line at the teller windows of the U.S. Treasury Department. Long lines would emerge. How long? How much time would people be willing to take from their leisure and their productive activities? A person whose time was worth $5 per hour would be willing to spend almost as much as ten hours waiting in line for the $50. But it might take longer than ten hours if there were enough others whose time was worth less—say, $3 or $4 per hour. And everyone would find that the waiting consumed much of the value of the $50 transfer. If the proponents thought the program would make the recipients $50 better off, they would have been wrong.

This simple example illustrates why the intended beneficiaries of transfer programs are not helped much. When beneficiaries have to do something (for example, wait in line, fill out forms, lobby government officials, take an exam, endure delays, or contribute to selected political campaigns) in order to qualify for a transfer, a great deal of their potential gain will be lost as they seek to meet the qualifying criteria. Similarly, when beneficiaries have to own something (for example, land with a wheat production history to gain access to wheat program subsidies, or a license to operate a taxicab or sell a product to foreigners) in order to get a subsidy, people will bid up the price of the asset needed to acquire the subsidy. The higher price of the asset, such as the taxicab license or the land with a history of wheat production, will capture the value of the subsidy.

In each case, the potential beneficiaries will compete to meet the criteria until they dissipate much of the value of the transfer. As a result, the recipient's *net gain* will generally be substantially less than the amount of the transfer payment. Indeed, the net gain of the *marginal* recipient (the person who barely finds it worthwhile to qualify for the transfer) will be very close, if not equal, to zero.

Transfer programs can even leave intended beneficiaries worse off. The Homestead Act of 1862 illustrates this point. Under this legislation, the federal government provided a land plot of 160 acres (later expanded to up to 640 acres in parts of the West) to settlers who staked their claim, built a house on the land, and stayed for five years. This option attracted many, but it was not easy to survive in the early West, even with 160 acres. Thus, more than 60 percent of the land claims were abandoned before the five years lapsed.[13] In essence, this transfer program encouraged people to settle the land before it was economical to do so, and many of the homesteaders paid a dear price trying to qualify for this subsidy. More recently, as we discussed in Part II, government regulations designed to make housing more affordable forced lenders to extend more loans with little or no down payment to home buyers who could not qualify for conventional mortgage loans. The impact of these regulatory subsidies was much like those of the Homestead Act: high default rates, foreclosures, and financial troubles for many of the intended beneficiaries.

There is a third reason for the ineffectiveness of transfers: Programs that protect potential recipients against adversity arising from their imprudent decisions encourage them to make choices that increase the likelihood of the adversity. Transfers do two things to potential beneficiaries: (1) they make the consequences of the adversity less severe, and (2) they reduce the incentive of potential recipients to take steps to avoid the adversity. The problem arises because these two things exert conflicting influences.

For example, government subsidies of insurance premiums in hurricane areas will reduce the *personal* cost for individuals to protect themselves against economic losses resulting from a hurricane. This increases their wealth. Because the subsidy makes the protection cheaper to them, however, more people will build in hurricane-prone areas and therefore the damage from hurricanes is greater than would otherwise be the case. Unemployment compensation provides another example. The benefits make it less costly for unemployed workers to refuse existing offers and keep looking for a better job. Therefore workers engage in longer periods of job search and, as a result, the unemployment rate is higher than it would be otherwise.[14]

With regard to poverty, the linkage between lifestyle choices and poverty is highly revealing. A recent study by Ron Haskins and Isabel Sawhill of the Brookings Institution found that a person can reduce his or her chances of living in poverty from 12 percent to 2 percent by doing just three basic things: completing high school (at a minimum), working full time, and getting married before having a child.[15] When young people choose these options, it is highly unlikely they will spend any significant time in poverty. This is a vitally important point that those of us in education need to communicate with our students, many of whom are making these life-changing decisions.

But adverse consequences accompany risky choices. The poverty rate of single-parent households is approximately five times the rate for two-parent households. Today, nearly 30 percent of children live in single-parent families, up from 12 percent in 1968. Among women under age 30, more than half of the births now occur outside of marriage. All of this confronts us with a dilemma: income transfers to the poor (e.g., food stamps, health care, housing, and cash payments) provide protection against the adverse consequences of poverty. But the transfers also encourage high-risk lifestyles (for example, dropping out of school or the workforce, childbearing by teenagers and unmarried women, divorce, abandonment of children by fathers, and drug use). As more people choose these high-risk lifestyles, it is very difficult to reduce the poverty rate. This is precisely what has happened during the past four decades.

Furthermore, government antipoverty transfers crowd out private charitable efforts by individuals, families, churches, and civic organizations. These private givers are more likely to see the real nature of the problem, be more sensitive to the lifestyles of recipients, and focus their giving on those making a good effort to help themselves and on those with a history of helping others. Thus private charitable efforts tend to be more effective than those undertaken by the government. In any case, when taxes are levied and the government does more, predictably, private individuals and groups will do less. As government antipoverty programs crowd out the more effective private programs, the problem worsens.

From an economic viewpoint, the failure of transfer programs ranging from farm price supports to antipoverty programs is not surprising. When the secondary effects are considered, economic analysis indicates that it is extremely difficult to help the intended beneficiaries over the long term.

8. Central Planning Replaces Markets with Politics, Which Wastes Resources and Retards Economic Progress.

The man of system is apt to be very wise in his own conceit. He seems to imagine that he can arrange the different members of a

*great society with as much ease as the hand arranges the different
pieces upon a chess-board; he does not consider that the pieces upon
the chess-board have not another principle of motion besides that
which the hand impresses upon them; but that, in the great chess-
board of human society, every single piece has a principle of motion of its own, although different from that which the legislature
might choose to impress upon it. If those two principles coincide
and act in the same direction, the game of human society will go on
easily and harmoniously, and is very likely to be happy and successful. If they are opposite or different, the game will go on miserably, and the society must be at all times in the highest degree of
disorder.*[16]

—ADAM SMITH (1759)

As previously discussed, governments can often coordinate the provision
of public goods—a small class of goods for which it is difficult to limit consumption to paying customers—better than markets. Many people also
believe that government officials can manage all, or most of, the economy
better than markets. The proponents of central planning believe that the
general populace would be better off if government officials used taxes,
subsidies, mandates, directives, and regulations to centrally plan and
manage the key sectors of the economy. Central planning replaces markets with government edicts. It can involve direct command and control,
as under the old Soviet system. But it can also occur when elected political officials substitute their verdicts for those of consumers, investors,
and entrepreneurs directed by market forces.

It is easy to see why central planning has a certain appeal to the nov-
ice. Surely it makes sense to plan. Aren't elected officials and government
experts more likely to represent the general welfare of the people than
business entrepreneurs? Won't government officials be less greedy than
private businesses? People who do not understand the invisible hand

principle often find the argument for central planning persuasive. Economics, however, indicates that it is wrong.

There are five major reasons why central planning will almost surely do more damage than good.

First, central planning merely substitutes politics for market verdicts. Real-world central planners (and the legislators who direct them) are not a group of omniscient selfless saints. Inevitably, the subsidies and investment funds doled out by planners will be influenced by political considerations.

Think how this process works even when decisions are made democratically. Expenditures will have to be approved by the legislature. Various business and unionized labor interests will lobby for investment funds and subsidies that provide them with benefits. Legislators will be particularly sensitive to those in a position to provide campaign contributions and deliver key voting blocs. Compared to newer growth firms, older established businesses will have a stronger record of political contributions, better knowledge of lobbying techniques, and a closer relationship with powerful political figures. As former Senator William Proxmire said: "The money will go where the political power is." The political process will favor older firms, even if they are economically weak, over newer growth-oriented firms. In addition, committee chairpersons will often block various programs unless other legislators agree to support projects beneficial to their constituents and favored interest groups (pork-barrel projects). Once these points are considered, only a dreamer could believe that this politicized process would result in less waste, more wealth creation, and a better allocation of investment funds than markets.

Second, the incentive of government-operated enterprises to keep costs low, be innovative, and efficiently supply goods is weak. Unlike private owners, the directors and managers of public-sector enterprises have little to gain from improved efficiency and lower costs. Predictably, they will be motivated to pursue a larger budget. A larger budget will provide funding for growth of the agency, salary increases, additional spending on clients, and other factors that will make life more comfortable for the managers. Managers of government enterprises and agencies, almost without exception, will try to convince the planners that their enterprises are producing goods or services that are enormously valuable to the general public and, if they were just given more funds, they would do even more marvelous things for society. Moreover, they will argue, if the funding is not forthcoming, people will suffer and the consequences will likely be disastrous.

It will often be difficult for legislators and other government planners to evaluate such claims. There is nothing comparable to private-sector profit rates that the planners can use to measure performance of the enterprise managers. In the private sector, bankruptcy eventually weeds out inefficiency, but in the public sector, there is no parallel mechanism for the termination of unsuccessful programs. In fact, poor performance and failure to achieve objectives is often used as an argument for *increased* government funding. The police department will use a rising crime rate to argue for additional law-enforcement funding. If the achievement scores of students are declining, public school administrators will use this failure to argue for still more funds. Given the strong incentive of government enterprise managers to expand their budgets, and the weak incentive to operate efficiently, government enterprises can be expected to have higher per-unit costs than comparable private firms.

Third, there is every reason to believe that investors risking their own money will make better investment choices than central planners spending the money of taxpayers. Remember, an investor who is going to profit must discover and invest in a project that increases the value of resources. The investor who makes a mistake—that is, whose investment project turns out to be a loser—will bear the consequences directly. In contrast, the success or failure of government projects seldom exerts much impact on the personal wealth of government planners. Even if a project is productive, the planner's personal gain is likely to be modest. Similarly, if the project is wasteful—if it reduces the value of resources— this failure will exert little negative impact on the income of planners. They may even be able to reap personal gain from wasteful projects that channel subsidies and other benefits toward politically powerful groups who will then give the bureau added political support at budget time. Given this incentive structure, there is no reason to believe that central planners will be more likely than private investors to discover and act on projects that increase society's wealth.

Fourth, the efficiency of government spending will also be undermined because the budget of an unconstrained government is something like a common pool resource. As we saw in Part II, Element 1, private ownership provides a strong motivation to take the future effects of current decisions into consideration. But when money and resources are commonly owned, there is little motivation to consider the future. For example, fish in the ocean are owned in common until someone catches them, and as a result, many species are on the verge of depletion because of overfishing. All fishermen would be better off if the fish were harvested less rapidly so there would be more opportunity for their reproduction and expansion of future population. But because of the common ownership, each fisherman knows that fish he does not catch today will be caught by someone else tomorrow. Thus, there is little incentive for anyone to reduce the catch today so more fish will be available in the future.

Similarly, when interest groups are "fishing" (lobbying political planners) for government spending, they have little incentive to consider the adverse consequences of higher taxes and additional borrowing on future output. The proponents of each spending project may recognize that future output would be greater if taxes were lower and private investment higher. But they will also figure if they do not grab more of the government budget, some other interest group will. Given this incentive structure, inefficient spending projects and perpetual budget deficits are an expected result in the era of unconstrained government. See the discussion in Part III, Element 5 on the problem of chronic government budget deficits.

Fifth, there is no way that central planners can acquire enough information to create, maintain, and constantly update a plan that makes sense. We live in a world of dynamic change. Technological advances, new products, political unrest, changing demand, and shifting weather conditions are constantly altering the relative scarcity of both goods and resources. No central authority will be able to keep up with these changes, politically assess them, and provide enterprise managers with sensible instructions.

Markets are different. Market prices register and tabulate widely fragmented information. Price information is constantly adjusting to reflect the changes always taking place in the economy. Prices reflect this widely dispersed information and send signals to business firms and resource suppliers. These price signals provide businesses and resource owners with the information required to coordinate their actions and bring them into harmony with the new conditions.

Some years ago it was widely believed that government planning and industrial policy provided the key to economic growth. We were told that market economies faced a dilemma: They were either going to have to move toward more government planning or suffer the consequences of slower growth and economic decline. Economists Paul Samuelson and Lester Thurow were among the leading proponents of this view, which dominated the popular media and sophisticated intellectual circles during the 1970s and 1980s. The collapse of the Soviet system and the poor performance of the Japanese economy have largely eroded the popularity of this view. Nonetheless, many still believe that the government can direct various sectors of the economy, such as health care and education. This, too, is a delusion.

Nearly two and a half centuries ago Adam Smith articulated the source of central-planning failures, including those that arise from efforts to plan specific sectors. (See the quote at the beginning of this element.) Unfortunately for government planners, individuals have minds of their own, what Smith calls "a principle of motion," and when they confront a personal incentive structure that encourages them to act in ways that conflict with the central plan, problems arise. When a government moves beyond its protective function and begins to subsidize various activities, operate enterprises, direct various sectors, and, in the extreme case, centrally plan the entire economy, invariably it will create a situation where individuals pursuing their own interest will simultaneously waste resources, undermine national prosperity, and cause living standards to fall well below their potential.

The record of government planning in the United States illustrates this point. It is fraught with conflicts and internal inconsistencies. The federal government pays some farmers *not* to produce grain products and, at the same time, provides others with subsidized irrigation projects so they can grow more of the very same grain products. Government programs for dairy farmers keep the price of milk high, while government subsidizes the school lunch program to make the expensive milk more affordable. Federal regulations mandating stronger bumpers make automobiles safer, while the Corporate Average Fuel Economy (CAFE) standards make them lighter and less safe. Both regulations increase the cost of automobiles and reduce the supply of cleaner, safer cars. The federal government sends aid to poor countries with the stated aim of helping them develop, but then it imposes import restrictions that limit the ability of these countries to help themselves (and

Americans, too) by supplying U.S. consumers with quality products at attractive prices.

Those who think that central planning, including the planning of sectors like health care and education, will promote economic progress are both arrogant and naive. When government officials decide what is bought and sold, or the prices of those items, the first thing that will be bought and sold will be the votes of elected officials. When enterprises get more funds from governments and less from consumers, they will spend more time trying to influence politicians and less time trying to reduce costs and please customers. Predictably, the substitution of politics for markets will lead to economic regression and, in the words of Adam Smith, "the game will go on miserably, and the society must be at all times in the highest degree of disorder."

9. Competition Is Just As Important in Government As in Markets.

Competition is a disciplinary force. In the marketplace, businesses must compete for the loyalty of customers. When firms serve their customers poorly, they generally lose business to rivals offering a better deal. Competition provides consumers with protection against high prices, shoddy merchandise, poor service, and/or rude behavior. Almost everyone recognizes this point with regard to the private sector. Unfortunately, the importance of competition in the public sector is not as widely recognized.

The incentives confronted by government agencies and enterprises are not very conducive to efficient operation. Unlike private owners, the directors and managers of public-sector enterprises are seldom in a position to gain much from lower costs and improved performance. In fact the opposite is often true. If an agency fails to spend this year's budget allocation, its case for a larger budget next year is weakened. Agencies typically go on a spending spree at the end of the budget period if they discover that they have failed to spend all of this year's appropriation.

In the private sector the profit rate provides an easily identifiable index of performance. Since there is no comparable indicator of performance in the public sector, managers of government firms can often gloss over economic inefficiency. In the private sector bankruptcy eventually weeds out inefficiency, but in the public sector there is no parallel mechanism for the termination of unsuccessful programs. In fact, as mentioned in the previous element, government agencies and enterprises often use deteriorating conditions and failure to achieve objectives as an argument for *increased* funding.

Given the incentives within the public sector, it is vitally important that government enterprises face competition. Private firms should be permitted to compete on a level playing field with government agencies and enterprises. When governments operate vehicle maintenance departments, printing shops, food services, garbage collection services, street maintenance departments, schools, and similar agencies, private firms can be given an equal opportunity to compete with public enterprises. For example, the U.S. Office of Management and Budget decided to see whether private printers could print the 2004 federal budget. Faced with competition, the Government Printing Office found that it could cut its price 23 percent. It kept the job by doing so. *Privatization Watch*—Reason Public Policy Institute's (RPPI) monthly newsletter—documents cases like this monthly at every level of government. Competition improves performance, reduces costs, and stimulates innovative behavior in government, as well as in the private sector. As a result, taxpayers get more for their money.

Competition among decentralized government units—state and local governments—also helps protect citizens from government exploitation. A government cannot be oppressive when citizens can easily choose the exit option—move to another location that provides a level of government services and taxes more to their liking. Of course it is not as easy to walk away from your government as from your grocer! In a decentralized setting, however, citizens can vote with their feet.

If the functions of the central government are strictly limited to the protection of individual rights, prohibition against restraints of trade, and the provision of national defense, then state and local governments can vary widely in the degree to which they levy taxes for the provision of government services. Just as people differ over how much they want to spend on housing or automobiles, so, too, will they have different views concerning expenditures on public services. Some will prefer higher levels of services and be willing to pay higher taxes for them. Others will prefer lower taxes and fewer governmental services. Some will want to fund government services with taxes, while others will prefer greater reliance on user charges. A decentralized system can accommodate and satisfy all of these divergent views.

Competition among governments will also promote governmental efficiency. If a government levies high taxes (without providing a parallel quality of service) and regulates excessively, individuals and businesses that make up their tax base will choose the exit option. Americans move a great deal, nearly 40 million each year. Moreover, their movements are not in a random pattern. Between 1998 and 2007, each year more than 4 million people moved away from the nine highest taxed states, including California, New York, New Jersey, Michigan, and Illinois. Most moved to lower tax states like Texas, Florida, Tennessee, Nevada, Utah, and Georgia.[17]

These movers are voting with their feet, and their actions are sending a message to high-tax, poorly run governments: *You need to change your ways because people do not like your policies.* Like businesses that realize losses when they fail to serve their customers, governments lose citizens when they serve them poorly. With decentralization, people will move toward governmental units that provide opportunity and desired public services at a low cost. In turn, the movements of voters will discipline governments and help keep them in line with the preferences of citizens.

If competition among decentralized governments is going to serve the interest of citizens, it must not be stifled by the policies of the federal government. When a central government subsidizes, mandates, and regulates the bundle of services provided by state and local governments, it undermines the competitive process among them. The best thing the central government can do is perform its limited functions well and remain neutral with regard to the operation and level of services of state, regional, and local governments.

Like private enterprises, units of government prefer protection from rivals. There will be a tendency for governments to seek a monopoly position. Therefore competition among governments will not evolve automatically. It will have to be incorporated into the political structure. This is precisely what the American founders were attempting to do when they designed the U.S. Constitution and the federal system of the United States.

10. Constitutional Rules That Bring the Political Process and Sound Economics into Harmony Will Promote Economic Progress.

> *The predominant teachings of this age are that there are no limits to man's capacity to govern others and that, therefore, no limitations ought to be imposed upon government. The older faith, born of long ages of suffering under man's dominion over man, was that the exercise of unlimited power by men with limited minds and self-regarding prejudices is soon oppressive, reactionary, and corrupt. Men may have to pass through a terrible ordeal before they find again the central truths they have forgotten. But they will find them again as they have so often found them again in other ages of reaction, if only the ideas that have misled them are challenged and resisted.*[18]
>
> —WALTER LIPPMANN

The intellectual folly of our age is the view that democratic elections alone will establish an environment conducive for economic progress. Beginning in elementary school, Americans are told that their elected representatives serve the interest of "all of the people" and that majority rule will lead to desired outcomes. But this is a fallacious view. The reality is quite different. As economic analysis of the political process indicates, elected legislators have a strong incentive to take resources from taxpayers and use them to provide favors to various voting blocs in exchange for political contributions, votes, and other forms of political support. When government moves beyond the protection of individual rights and becomes heavily involved in the allocation of scarce resources, favored treatment of selected groups, at the expense of others, replaces equal treatment under the law.

The Senate passage of a 2,000-page healthcare bill in December of 2009 provided a vivid illustration of how the political process really works. A senator from Louisiana delivered her vote in exchange for $300 million of Medicaid benefits for her state. A senator from Nebraska "sold" his vote for permanent federal funding of Medicaid for his state and a special tax exemption for Mutual of Omaha, a large Nebraska-based health insurer. A Florida senator provided enthusiastic support after the bill incorporated special treatment of Medicare Advantage for Floridians. Labor unions were granted a special exemption from the taxation of high-benefit medical insurance plans. The list of differential treatment and special favors went on and on. Even the pretense of equal treatment under the law was abandoned. While the process was not atypical, the inside deals and political favoritism were more visible than is usually the case. The experience was a powerful civics lesson for Americans, and it may well have awakened many to the truth about government planning and political allocation.

When government is unconstrained, political democracy will lead to excessive debt and excessive spending driven by exploitation of the taxpayer by favor-seeking interest groups. Divisive and predatory activities will proliferate. Individuals will spend more time organizing and fighting over slices of the economic pie and less time producing "pie." As a result, output will be smaller than would otherwise be the case. Moreover, distrust, animosity among factions, and political corruption will grow, while production stagnates. Life in a highly politicized economy is not a pretty scene.

Many people believe that America has already traveled too far down the road to collectivism and political control to turn back. We disagree. Others have done so. After four decades of expanding government and economic stagnation that was widely referred to as the British disease, the United Kingdom turned back during the 1980s. New Zealand turned back during the late 1980s and early 1990s. Ireland also reversed its big government course in the late 1980s when it confronted slow growth, loss of population, and a plunging credit rating. The politicization of the U.S. economy is no worse today than in the 1930s. The inflation, high unemployment, price controls, and monetary instability of the 1970s was also a difficult era. But this period of excessive government was followed by a time of relatively sound governmental policies, thus generating two decades of both growth and stability. As the above quote from one of the twentieth century's most renowned journalists, Walter Lippmann, indicates, people may forget central truths, but they will find them again if the ideas that misled them are challenged.

If government is going to be a positive force for economic prosperity, the rules of the political game must bring the self-interest of voters, politicians, and bureaucrats into harmony with economic progress. Limited government, federalism, and equal treatment under the law are central to the achievement of this objective.

Basically, the framers of the U.S. Constitution got the general structure right. They limited the powers of the central government and provided for free trade among the states. The framers enumerated the permissible fiscal powers of the central government (Article I, Section 8) and allocated all other powers to the states and the people (Tenth Amendment). They also prohibited states from adopting legislation "impairing the obligation of contracts" (Article I, Section 10). Furthermore, the Fifth Amendment specifies that private property shall not be "taken for public use without just compensation." Congress was to levy uniform taxes in order "to provide for the common defense and general welfare." The clear intent was to prevent the use of the federal treasury as a tool to favor some groups and regions relative to others. Legislation had to pass through two legislative bodies that, at the time, represented diverse and often conflicting interests and acquire the approval of the president before it became law. Political power was divided among the legislative, executive, and judicial branches. The limitations on the powers of the central government provided for a federal system and still more dispersal of governmental powers. Clearly, the U.S. Constitution sought to limit the ability of government, particularly the federal government, to politicize the economy and abrogate the rights of citizens.

Put another way, the constitution was designed to promote government action based on agreement rather than coercion. Why is this important? People will agree to an action only when each gains. Thus, actions based on agreement, whether undertaken through markets or government, will be mutually advantageous and will therefore promote the general welfare rather than the interests of some parties at the expense of others.

With the passage of time, the constraints of the original Constitution eroded. The federal government is now involved in almost everything and the results are highly visible: political favoritism, special-interest spending, large budget deficits, excessive regulation, political corruption, and increased influence over many aspects of our lives. The challenge before us is to restore the intent of the constitutional rules and to develop a few new ones that will promote government action based on agreement and bring the political process back into harmony with economic progress.

A Positive Program for Prosperity

How can this be accomplished? What provisions would a constitution designed to promote economic prosperity and stability contain? Several proposals flow directly from our analysis. Within the American context, we believe that the following eight provisions would provide the core for an Economic Bill of Rights that would promote economic progress.

a. *Neither the federal government nor state and local*
    governments shall use their regulatory powers to take
    private property, either partially or in its entirety, for public
    use without paying the owner the full market value
    of the claimed property.

Court decisions have eroded the protection of private property provided by the Fifth Amendment. In recent years, state and local governments have used regulations to take or control private property without compensation, even though the property owner had violated the rights of no one. Moreover, court decisions have permitted state and local governments to take property from one party and then transfer it to another. This is an action that clearly conflicts with the intent of the "public use" provision of the Fifth Amendment. Courts have generally allowed such takings of private property as long as a legislative body deemed that the action was "in the public interest," or that the taking did not deny the owner all uses of his or her property. These are open doors for the abuse of private property rights that must be closed, and the Fifth Amendment should be revised to close them.

b. *The right of individuals to compete in a business or*
    profession and/or buy and sell legally tradable goods
    and services at mutually acceptable terms shall not be
    infringed by Congress or any of the States.[19]

The freedom of individuals to compete in business and engage in voluntary exchange activities is a cornerstone of both economic freedom and progress. Price controls, business and occupational entry restraints,[20] laws restricting the exchange of goods and services across state boundaries, and other government regulations that restrain trade should be prohibited.

c. *Congress shall not levy taxes or impose quotas on either imports or exports.*

The U.S. Constitution already prohibits the imposition of these trade restraints on exports. This prohibition should also be extended to imports. The freedom to trade is a basic human right, just like freedom of speech and freedom of religion. There is no reason why Americans should not be permitted to buy from, and sell to, whoever will give them the best deal, even if the trading partner lives in another country.

d. *A constraint on the total level of federal spending must be imposed and the budget process should begin with the establishment of this constraint.*

The federal budget process does not have a total spending constraint. As a result, federal spending is far beyond the optimal level, favor-seeking interests groups enrich themselves at the expense of the disorganized taxpayer, and numerous counterproductive programs reduce our potential income. A constitutional budget constraint should be imposed. It should be placed on spending because total expenditure is the best indicator of the burden of government. Households, businesses, and even state and local governments confront budget constraints. So, too, should the federal government.

There are several ways this might be done. One would be to adopt a constitutional amendment limiting federal spending to 20 percent of GDP, approximately the average of the past fifty years. Another would be to adopt a constitutional requirement that the president include a total spending constraint in his annual budget proposal submitted to Congress and then require three-fourths approval of both House and Senate to override this spending constraint. This would hold a single person, the only one elected by all voters, responsible for the total spending level, so there would be no doubt who is accountable for out-of-control spending.

Still another way to establish the spending constraint would be to integrate a form into the federal personal income tax that would allow the votes of those paying this tax to determine whether federal spending during the upcoming fiscal year should be reduced, remain the same, or expanded. This alternative would have the advantage of permitting those paying for the spending to determine its level. Again, this spending constraint could be overridden only by a three-fourths vote of both legislative branches and approval by the president. People who do not pay taxes should not be permitted to enrich themselves by taking the property of those who do. Neither should politicians be allowed to take the income property of taxpayers and use it to "buy" the votes of non-taxpayers. Allowing taxpayers to set the overall spending constraint would reduce both of these perverse incentives.[21]

The United States is now approaching the situation where 50 percent of the voters pay no personal income tax. Unless those who pay taxes are provided with additional protection, government will increasingly resemble a barroom brawl and our living standards will be eroded as groups compete for special treatment by the government. The federal budgetary process is broken. Steps need to be taken to force legislators to more fully confront the opportunity costs of government spending. Establishment of a meaningful budget constraint is the only way that goal can be achieved.

e. *A three-fourths approval of both Houses of Congress shall be required for all expenditure programs of the federal government. At least two-thirds approval of the legislative branches of state government shall be required for the approval of expenditures by state governments.*

This provision is designed to strengthen federalism and correct the tendency of power and control to flow toward the central government. The supermajority requirements for approval at the federal and state levels will mean that broad agreement, not just a majority, will be required before a project can be undertaken at these levels. This will reduce the prevalence of counterproductive projects that squander resources. If a project is really productive, there will always be a method of finance that will result in everyone's gaining. Thus, the supermajority provisions need not eliminate projects that truly increase wealth. They will, however, make it more difficult for special interests to use government as a tool for plunder. They will also help direct the spending activities of governments to the local level, where competition among governments provides a stronger incentive to serve the interests of all citizens.

f. A three-fourths approval of both Houses of Congress
shall be required for the federal government to run an
annual budget deficit or raise the overall limit
on the national debt.

As recent history illustrates, Congress is addicted to deficit spending. The current limit on the federal debt level is not a serious restraint, because every time the public debt ceiling is approached, a simple majority of Congress raises the limit. A constitutional provision requiring three-fourths approval for both budget deficits and a revision in the debt limit would help Congress control its spending and borrowing addictions.

g. A three-fourths approval of both Houses of Congress
shall be required for the federal government to mandate
any expenditures by either state governments or private
business firms.

If this provision is not included, Congress will use mandated expenditures to escape the prior spending and borrowing limitations.

h. *The function of the Federal Reserve System is to maintain the value of the currency and establish a stable price level. If the price level either increases or decreases by more than 4 percent annually during two consecutive years, all governors of the Federal Reserve System shall be required to submit their resignations.*

This provision would make it clear what the Fed is supposed to do. If the Fed establishes monetary stability, it is doing its part to promote economic stability and progress.

These provisions would enhance the protection of private ownership rights, promote competition, strengthen federalism, and help bring government spending and borrowing under control, while limiting the inclination of politicians to serve special-interest groups.[22] They would be a positive step toward the restoration of government based on mutual agreement rather than the power to plunder. We have no doubt that they would assure growth and prosperity for future generations of Americans.

Before constitutional rules consistent with economic progress can be reestablished, however, the intellectual fabric underlying the case for limited government based on agreement rather than coercion must be mended. We must cast aside the myth that popular elections are the distinctive feature of the American political process. We must recognize that it is one thing to determine our political leaders by majority vote and quite another to determine what government will do by majority rule. When the government focuses only on those activities that provide broad public net benefits, it will gain more respect and thus be stronger. Limited government, not majority rule, is the key to both economic progress and a government that earns the respect of its citizens. The sooner we learn this important point, the more free and prosperous we will be.

Concluding Thoughts

Both basic economics and the American experience shed considerable insight on the wealth of nations and the sources of economic progress. As we explained in Part II, private ownership, freedom of exchange, competitive markets, the rule of law, and monetary stability are the cornerstones of prosperity. When these cornerstones are present, individuals will be able to "reap what they sow," productive energy will be unleashed, and wealth will be created. This is the recipe that generated America's economic progress and improved its standard of living. To the degree that America departs from it, America will experience reduced growth and prosperity.

Parts II and III focused on national prosperity. The final section of this book will focus on personal prosperity by considering some practical choices you can make that will help you achieve a more prosperous life.

PART IV

*Twelve Key Elements
of Practical Personal Finance*

TWELVE KEY ELEMENTS OF
PRACTICAL PERSONAL FINANCE

1. Discover your comparative advantage.

2. Be entrepreneurial. In a market economy, people get ahead by helping others and discovering better ways of doing things.

3. Use budgeting to help you save regularly and spend your money more effectively.

4. Don't finance anything for longer than its useful life.

5. Two ways to get more out of your money: Avoid credit-card debt and consider purchasing used items.

6. Begin paying into a "real-world" savings account every month.

7. Put the power of compound interest to work for you.

8. Diversify—don't put all of your eggs in one basket.

9. Indexed equity funds can help you beat the experts without taking excessive risk.

10. Invest in stocks for long-run objectives, but as the need for money approaches, increase the proportion of bonds.

11. Beware of investment schemes promising high returns with little or no risk.

12. Teach your children how to earn money and spend it wisely.

Introduction

Compared to Americans a couple of generations ago and their contemporaries worldwide, today's Americans have incredibly high income levels. Yet many are under financial stress. How can this be? The answer is that financial insecurity is mainly the result of the choices we make, not the incomes we earn.

If you do not take charge of your finances, they will take charge of you. As Yogi Berra, the great American philosopher (and former baseball star), said, "You've got to be very careful if you don't know where you are going, because you might not get there." In other words, each of us needs a plan. If we don't have one, we may end up where we do not want to be. The twelve elements below form the core of a practical plan. Like the rest of this book, they are directed toward the interested layperson, not to specialists. They focus on practical suggestions—things that you can begin doing immediately—that will help you make better financial decisions whatever your current age, income level, or health status.

Often, personal finance and investment decisions seem totally divorced from the world of economics. But they are not. As we will see, the principle of comparative advantage, which explains why countries benefit from specializing in the activities they do best, also explains why you as an individual can benefit from specialization in things you do well that are valued highly by others. Similarly, when it comes to building wealth over time, entrepreneurship, financial accountability, career planning, and investment in capital (especially human capital) are as valuable for individuals as they are for countries.

We are not trying to make you a Wall Street wizard or an instant millionaire. The advice presented here deals with financial basics and common sense. Some of the points may seem obvious; others may surprise you; but all are supported by logic and experience. This plan is not the most comprehensive available, and it may not be the best financial plan for you. But the search for perfection is often the enemy of positive action. Individuals who think they don't have the time or the expertise to develop a sound financial plan may fail even to apply simple guidelines that can help them avoid financial troubles or even disaster. This section will give you such guidelines. Embrace them.

Before suggesting ways to make better financial decisions and get more from the resources available to you, we want to share a couple of thoughts about the importance of money and wealth. First, there is more to a good life than making money. When it comes to happiness, nonfinancial assets such as a good marriage, family, friends, self-fulfilling work, religious convictions, and enjoyable hobbies are far more important than money. Thus the single-minded pursuit of money and wealth makes no sense.

At the same time, however, there is nothing unseemly about the desire for more wealth. This desire is not limited to those who are only interested in their personal welfare, narrowly defined. For example, the late Mother Teresa would have liked more wealth so that she could have done more to help the poor. Many people would like more wealth so they can donate more to religious, cultural, and charitable organizations, or do more to help elderly parents. No matter what our objectives in life, they are easier to achieve if we have less debt and more wealth. Thus all of us have an incentive to improve our financial decision-making. This section will offer twelve guidelines to help us do so.

1. Discover Your Comparative Advantage.

The principle of comparative advantage is most often used to explain why free trade makes it possible for people in different countries to produce larger outputs and achieve higher living standards. As we saw in Element 4 of Part I, two countries can each gain by trading with each other, even if one country is the best at producing everything and another is the worst at producing everything. The principle of comparative advantage is just as important to the wealth of individuals. Finding the occupational or business activity in which you have a comparative advantage and specializing in it will help you earn more money than otherwise, regardless of how good you are in absolute terms.

Like nations, individuals will be able to achieve higher income levels when they specialize—that is, concentrate their efforts on those things that they do best. To pick one extreme, suppose that you are better than everyone else in every productive activity. Would that mean that you should try to spend some time on each activity? Or to go to another extreme, someone could be worse than everyone else. Would that individual be unable to gain from specialization because he or she would be unable to compete successfully in anything? The answer to both questions is no. No matter how talented you are, you will be *relatively* more productive in some areas than others. Similarly, no matter how poor your ability to produce things, you will still have a comparative advantage in something; you will be able to compete successfully in some things and can gain by specializing in your comparative advantage (see Element 4 of Part I for additional information on comparative advantage).

In other words, your comparative advantage is determined by your comparative abilities, not your absolute abilities. For example, Oprah Winfrey has the skills not only to be one of the world's best talk show hosts and producers, but she also has what it takes to be one of the world's best entertainment agents. Who could do a better job than Oprah in helping you make the right contacts in the entertainment business, informing you about who could do the most to help you develop your talents and how to make the best first impression? But Oprah has a comparative advantage in hosting talk shows and producing other media events, not in being an entertainment agent. She would be giving up far more value as an entertainment agent than she gives up by hosting and producing variety entertainment; that is, her opportunity cost in the former occupation is far greater than her opportunity cost in the latter. Similarly, most of those working as entertainment agents may have less talent than Oprah would bring to that occupation, but since their skills as agents are far better than their skills as talk show hosts and producers, they sacrifice less value working as agents than they would working as talk show hosts and producers, so their comparative advantages lie in being agents.

Individuals will always be better off if they are really good at something that is highly valued by others. This explains why people like Oprah make a lot of money, and why Oprah herself is one of the wealthiest women in the United States. She is regularly placed high on the annual *Forbes* magazine list of the four hundred richest Americans. But even a person who is not very good at anything will be better off by specializing where his or her disadvantage is smallest compared to others and by trading with others who have different specialties.

Some people may feel that they are at a disadvantage when they trade with others who earn far more money. But remember that trade benefits both parties. And generally, the more accomplished and wealthy the people you trade with (and working for someone is the same as trading with them), the better off you are because your service is typically worth more to them than to those who are less accomplished and wealthy. If we were entertainment agents we would rather work for Oprah than for any other media star because we would almost surely make more money that way.

The worst thing you can do is convince yourself, or be convinced by others, that you are somehow a victim and therefore unable to become wealthy through your own effort and initiative. Some people start out with fewer advantages than others, but as we will see, even those who are less advantaged can do extremely well financially if they make the effort and apply themselves intelligently. You need to take charge of your career development and plan how you can best develop your talents and use market cooperation to achieve your goals. No one else cares more about your personal success than you do. Nor does anyone else know more about your interests, skills, and goals.

We usually perceive of costs as something that should be kept as low as possible. But remember, costs reflect the highest valued opportunity given up when we choose an option. Thus, when you have attractive alternatives, your choices will be costly. Furthermore, as you improve your skills and your opportunities become even more attractive, the choice of an option will be still more costly. In contrast, your costs will be low when you have very few good choices. For example, a very effective way of reducing the cost of reading this book is to get thrown in jail with it so that reading it is the only opportunity you have other than staring at the walls. This is obviously a bad idea. It would reduce the cost of doing one thing (although a very desirable thing in our opinion) by eliminating your opportunity to do many other desirable things. You make yourself better off by increasing your opportunities, not by reducing them.

Young people are encouraged to get a good education so they will have more attractive opportunities later in life. But this is the same as encouraging them to increase the costs of all the choices they make. A good education increases your productivity and the amount employers are willing to pay you. This will improve your income, but it also means you will have to turn down some attractive offers. A good education also enhances your appreciation of a host of pastimes such as listening to good music, reading fine literature, and experiencing the beauty of the world's natural wonders. This heightens your enjoyment and deepens the meaning of your life, but it does so by increasing the opportunity cost of choosing one leisure-time activity over another.

Sound career decision making involves more than figuring out those things that you do best. It is also vitally important to discover where your passions lie—those productive activities that provide you with the most fulfillment. If you enjoy what you do and believe it is important, you will be happy to do more of it and work to do it better. Thus, competency and passion for an activity tend to go together. Moreover, real wealth is measured in terms of personal fulfillment. For example, the authors of this book (all economists) have found it satisfying to find answers to economic questions and to express what we know in ways that can help others better understand the little corners of the world—and in some cases parts of the big picture, too—that we have examined professionally. Even though the hours are sometimes long, we find most of those hours enjoyable. What we do is not for everyone. But for us, with our interests, the joys of what we do more than make up for the rough patches.

2. Be Entrepreneurial. In a Market Economy, People Get Ahead by Helping Others and Discovering Better Ways of Doing Things.

Entrepreneurship involves choices about how to use resources. While the term is often associated with decision making in business, in a very real sense all of us are entrepreneurs. We are constantly making decisions about the development and use of knowledge, skills, and other resources under our control. Our financial success will reflect the outcome of these choices.

If you want to be financially successful, you need to think entrepreneurially. Put another way, you need to focus on how you can develop and use your talents and available resources to provide others with things that they value highly.

Providing others with goods and services that are highly valued compared to their cost is the key to financial success. Consider the hypothetical case of Robert Jones, a land developer. Jones purchases large land tracts, subdivides them, and adds various amenities such as roads, sewage disposal, golf courses, and parks. Jones will profit if he is able to sell the plots for more than the cost of the land and the various amenities he has constructed. If his actions are profitable, they will increase the value of the resources and help others by providing them with better home sites than are available elsewhere. Jones's financial success or failure is dependent on his ability to enhance the value of resources.

Sometimes entrepreneurial activity is much less complex than this. For example, fifteen-year-old Henry, who purchases a power mower and sells lawn services to neighbors, is also an entrepreneur. He is seeking to profit by increasing the value of resources—his time and equipment. Simplicity does not change the key to entrepreneurial success. Just as in the case of Jones, Henry's success will depend on his ability to use resources in a way that increases their value to others.

Individuals who focus their brainpower on how they can provide goods and services that others value highly will have a major advantage in the marketplace. Many employees spend time thinking about how much they are getting paid rather than how they can make their services more valuable to both current and prospective employers. Similarly, many business owners focus on management details rather than on increasing the value of their product or service relative to its cost. But financial success is about making your services more valuable to others. Both employees and employers who focus on this factor will enhance their likelihood of success.

Once you begin to think entrepreneurially—to think about how you can increase the value of your services to others—do not underestimate your ability to achieve success. Entrepreneurial talent is often found in unexpected places. Who would have thought that a middle-aged milkshake-machine salesman, Ray Kroc, would revolutionize the franchising business and expand a single McDonald's restaurant in San Bernardino,

California, into the world's largest fast-food chain? Did anyone expect Sam Walton, the operator of just a couple of small stores in one of the nation's poorest states in 1970, to become the largest retailer in America during the 1990s? How could anyone have anticipated that Ted Turner, the owner of an outdoor sign business in Atlanta, whose rowdy behavior had led to his expulsion from Brown University, would develop one of the world's largest cable news networks, CNN?

These are high-profile cases, but the same pattern occurs over and over. Successful business and professional leaders often come from diverse backgrounds that appear to be largely unrelated to the areas of their achievement. But they have one thing in common: They are good at discovering better ways of doing things and strategically acting on opportunities to increase the value of resources that have generally been overlooked by others.

Entrepreneurs, who are mostly self-employed, are disproportionately represented among America's millionaires. Statistically the self-employed constitute less than a fifth of the workforce, but they account for two-thirds of the millionaires. And self-employed millionaires tend to achieve their millionaire status at an earlier age.

The financial success of self-employed entrepreneurs stems from four major factors.

First and foremost, their success reflects entrepreneurial talent: an ability to discover innovative new products, cost-reducing production methods, and profitable opportunities that have been overlooked by others.

Second, self-employment is more risky than working at a job, and greater risk and higher returns go together. Self-employment is risky. Other things constant, people prefer less risk. If the incomes of the self-employed were not higher, people would be unwilling to accept the risks and uncertainties of this occupation. Thus, to a degree, the higher incomes of the self-employed are merely compensation for the uncertainties accompanying this form of employment.

Third, a high savings rate often adds to the wealth of entrepreneurs. Self-employed business owners often take very little income out of the business initially for consumption. Rather, they invest more in establishing and growing their business. Even after it has grown and is successful, the owners often put much of the profits into improvement and further expansion.

Fourth, business owners typically work long hours. For many self-employed entrepreneurs, a forty-hour workweek would seem like a spring break. These more lengthy hours of work also enhance their income and wealth.

Employees, too, can adopt the characteristics that contribute to the high-income status and wealth of self-employed entrepreneurs. They can channel their savings into stocks and thereby achieve the above-average returns that come with the risk of business ownership. If they desire, they can also generate more income and accumulate more wealth through higher rates of saving and more hours of work. Perhaps most important, employees can gain by "thinking like entrepreneurs." Just as the incomes of business entrepreneurs depend on their ability to satisfy customers, the earnings of employees depend on their ability to make themselves valuable to employers, both current and prospective. If employees want to achieve high earnings, they need to develop talents, skills, and work habits that are highly valued by others.

This entrepreneurial way of thinking is particularly important when making decisions about education and training. Education will not enhance your earnings very much unless you get knowledge and develop skills that make your services more valuable to others. These include the ability to write well, to communicate well at the individual level, and to use basic math tools, as well as specific skills that can set you apart from the crowd and raise your productivity. Developing skills that make you more valuable to others is a key to education at both the high school and college level. College students who believe that a degree by itself is a ticket to a high-paying job often experience a rude awakening when they enter the job market.

In a market economy, both business owners and employees get ahead by discovering better ways of doing things and helping others in exchange for income. If you want to have a high income, you need to figure out how you can develop and use your talents in ways that provide large benefits to others.

3. Use Budgeting to Help You Save Regularly and Spend Your Money More Effectively.

> "'My other piece of advice, Copperfield,' said Mr. Micawber, 'you know. Annual income twenty pounds, annual expenditure nineteen six, result happiness. Annual income twenty pounds, annual expenditure twenty pounds ought and six, result misery.'"
>
> —CHARLES DICKENS, *David Copperfield*

Most financial insecurity today is the consequence of poor saving, lack of budgeting, and other unwise financial habits. Both saving and budgeting are crucial to building wealth. People, like nations, become wealthy by saving regularly—consuming less than they earn or produce. Only by saving can an individual or a country accumulate the capital that is necessary to generate wealth. But it takes more than just accumulating capital. There must be a plan of strategic action behind it. That plan is a budget. It will help you get the most out of your income while saving regularly and spending wisely. Four simple steps will help you achieve financial success: motivate yourself, set financial goals, create a budget, and put a plan into action today.

Step 1. Change your personal spending behavior and use savings to contribute to wealth building. If you do not start now, it is unlikely that you will do so later. Don't fool yourself into believing that saving is easier when you earn more money. True, people do save more as incomes increase. But high incomes are usually a result of early savings and creative budgeting. People with strong saving habits generally started saving early when their incomes were much lower.[1] They put their savings to work for them and tapped into the power of compound interest. More is provided on this in Element 7.

It is easy to procrastinate. But almost everyone, even those with small incomes, can find ways to spend and save strategically. Commit to creating a budget that plans your spending, provides emergency funds, helps you meet various financial goals, and supplies funds for investing. A well-crafted budget can help you increase financial security today and build wealth in the future. Now that you are motivated, let's discuss setting financial goals.

Step 2. Set goals. Incentives matter. So put them to work for you. Set financial goals and incorporate them into your budget. Separate them into short-, medium-, and long-term goals. Short-term goals can be achieved within the next year and provide immediate gratification. Shed some credit-card debt, buy the world's lightest netbook, increase your savings for rainy day expenses, set money aside for insurance, or purchase a nice gift for someone. Midterm goals are achieved over a longer period— anywhere between one and three years. Purchasing a new car with cash, putting 20 percent down on a home or condo, and building a solid savings account leading to a well-diversified portfolio require more present-day sacrifices for future gains. Finally, saving and investing for college, retirement, and paying off a home mortgage are goals that will take longer to achieve.

Step 3. Devise a plan of action: Create a personal budget with actual and proposed items to achieve your financial goals. Although we are constantly thinking about all the things we "need" to buy, we buy more than we really have to have. The best way to see where you can begin a savings program while achieving your financial goals is by budgeting. A list of your expected income amounts over a period of time in the future, and how you plan to allocate each dollar of that income (a budget), lets you examine systematically how you are using your monthly disposable income. By making clear to yourself how much income you have and how it can best be used, a budget allows you to highlight expenditures that you can reduce, or eliminate entirely, and hardly notice. At the same time, it will draw attention to opportunities to save and invest more. Figure out your monthly basics—show how much you earn, spend, save, pay in taxes and face in fixed and variable expenses. It is relatively easy and numerous resources are available at your fingertips. Visit CommonSenseEconomics.com for budgeting basics and suggestions on creative consumption and savings.

Step 4. Take the plunge! Begin a savings and investment program now to meet your financial goals. Obviously the sooner you start saving and spending strategically, the more wealth you will have by retirement. What is not so obvious is how much more retirement wealth you can accumulate by starting early. Even the smallest amount saved or invested today can make a very big difference in building future wealth. Consider the following plan.

Start regularly saving $2 a day for two years when you turn twenty-two years of age. That's probably not as much as you will spend on coffee, bottled water, snacks or have in loose change at the end of the day. Then from your twenty-fourth until your twenty-sixth birthday, begin saving $3 a day. That's just a dollar more and your income will probably have increased. Between the ages of twenty-six and thirty, bump up your savings amount to $4 per day. By not spending this amount daily and putting it aside in an account with a positive rate of return, you won't cramp your style much. By the time you reach thirty, you will have saved $9,490, plus the interest received—quite a nice sum. Saving $2, $3, or $4 a day really adds up.

But here's the real surprise. By the time you retire at age sixty-seven, that early start can easily add $153,305 to your wealth if invested wisely, and that's in today's purchasing power. All you have to do is receive a rate of return equal to about what the stock market has yielded over the last eight decades (more on this rate of return later), and the dollars saved each day will be a fairly small percentage of your total accumulated wealth at retirement if you really do keep saving from age thirty on. Also keep in mind that you are far more likely to *continue* saving at thirty than to *start* at thirty.

So next time you are thinking about all the things you "need," recognize that you do not really have to have many of them. Remember that spending today costs you in terms of your future wealth. We aren't suggesting that you live a life of deprivation so you can be rich in the future. That makes no sense. But there are many creative ways to reduce spending and increase saving. Budgeting and laying out a savings plan will produce immediate satisfaction, help you gain a sense of financial control and security and build wealth for the future. *When it comes to starting, the best rule is: "Just do it."*

Elements 4 through 11 provide more details on how to avoid overspending and excessive debt, get the most out of your money, invest strategically, and steer clear of unwise investment schemes.

4. Don't Finance Anything for Longer Than Its Useful Life.

What happens when you borrow money to purchase vacations, clothing, or other goods that are quickly consumed or that depreciate in value? What happens when you take out a forty-eight-month loan in order to purchase a used automobile that will be worn out in two years? The answer to both questions is the same: You will soon be making payments on things that have little or no value to you or anyone else. These payments will lead to frustration, bitterness, and financial insecurity.

Financing an item over a time period more lengthy than the useful life of the asset forces you to pay in the future both for your past pleasure *and* your current desires. This also leads easily to spending more than you earn, which means your indebtedness will increase and you will become poorer and poorer in the future. This is the route to financial disaster.

Does it ever make sense for an individual or family to purchase a good on credit? The answer is yes, but only if the good is a long-lasting asset and if the borrowed funds are repaid before the asset is worn out. This way you pay for a good as you use it.

Very few purchases meet these criteria. Three major expenditures come to mind: housing, automobiles, and education. If maintained properly, a new house may provide useful life for forty or fifty years into the future. Under these circumstances, the use of a thirty-year mortgage to finance the expenditure is perfectly sensible. Similarly, if an automobile can reasonably be expected to be driven five or six years, there's nothing wrong with financing it over a time period of forty-eight months or less. And like housing, investments in education generally provide net benefits over a lengthy time period. Young people investing in a college education can expect to reap dividends in the form of higher earnings over the next thirty or forty years of their life. The higher earnings will provide the means for the repayment of educational loans. When long-lasting assets are still generating additional income or a valuable service after the loans used to finance their purchase are repaid, some of the loan payments are actually a form of savings and investment and will enhance the net worth of a household.

For most households the implications of this guideline are straightforward: Do not borrow funds to finance anything other than housing, automobiles, and education. Furthermore, make sure that funds borrowed for the purchase of these items will be repaid well before the expiration of the asset's useful life. Application of this simple guideline will go a long way toward keeping you out of financial trouble.

5. Two Ways to Get More Out of Your Money: Avoid Credit-Card Debt and Consider Purchasing Used Items.

Most of us would like to have more in the future without having to give up much today. Many, including those with incomes well above average, do two things that undermine this objective. First, they go into debt to buy things before they can afford them. Second, they insist on buying new items even when used ones would be just as serviceable and far more economical.

Imprudent use of credit cards can be a huge stumbling block to financial success. Although many people are careful with cards, others act as if an unused balance on a credit card is like money in the bank. This is blatantly false. An unused balance on your credit card merely means that you have some additional borrowing power; it does not enhance your wealth or provide you with more money. It is best to think of your credit card as an extension of your checking account. If you have funds in your checking account, you can use your credit card to access those funds—if you pay off the bill every month. If you don't have sufficient funds in your account, don't make the purchase.

While credit cards are convenient to use, they are also both seductive and a costly method of borrowing. Because credit cards make it easy to run up debt, they are potentially dangerous. Some people seem unable to control the impulse to spend when there is an unused balance on their cards.[2] If you have this problem you need to take immediate action! You need to get your hands on a pair of scissors and cut up all of your credit cards. If you do not, they will lead to financial misfortune.

Charging purchases on your credit card makes it look as though you are buying more with your money, but the bill invariably comes at the end of the month. This presents another temptation: the option to send in a small payment to cover the interest and a tiny percentage of the balance and keep most of your money to spend on more things. If you choose this option and continue to run up your balance, however, you will quickly confront a major problem—the high interest rates being charged on the unpaid balance.

It is common for people to pay as much as 15 to 18 percent on their credit-card debt. This is far higher than most people, even successful investors, can earn on their savings and investments. As we shall see in later elements, you can easily become wealthy earning 7 percent per year on your savings. Unfortunately, high interest rates on outstanding debt will have the opposite impact. Paying 15 to 18 percent on your credit-card debt can drive even a person with a good income into poverty.

Consider the example of Sean, a young professional who decides to take a few days relaxing in the Bahamas. The trip costs Sean $1,500, which he puts on his credit card. But instead of paying the full amount at the end of the month, Sean pays only the minimum, and he keeps doing so for the next ten years, when the bill is finally paid off. How much did Sean pay for his trip, assuming an 18 percent interest rate on his credit card? He pays $26.63 per month for 120 months, or a total of $3,195.40. So Sean pays his credit-card company more for the trip than he paid for the air travel, hotel rooms, food, and entertainment.

Sean could have taken the trip for a whole lot less by planning ahead and starting to make payments to himself before the trip instead of making payments to the credit-card company after the trip. By saving $75 a month at 5 percent per year in compound interest (we will discuss compound interest in Element 7) for twenty months, Sean could have had $1,560.89 for the trip, and not the $3,195.40 he ended up paying (including interest) for the same trip (but taken earlier) on the credit card. In other words, by saving and planning to make his trip, instead of running up credit-card debt to pay for it, Sean could take two trips (with extra spending money) for less than what he ended up paying for one on credit.

Or better yet, Sean could have had the trip for $1,500, and then, instead of paying the credit-card company $26.63 per month for the next ten years, he could put that amount in savings. If he does and earns 5 percent per year, he will end up with $4,135.26 at the end of the ten years. At that point he can spend $2,000 on another trip and still have $2,135.26 left over. It is obvious from this example, and any number of others that we could give, that those who try to increase their consumption using credit-card debt end up having less consumption and less money than those who avoid credit-card debt and save instead.

Of course, you may already have a sizable credit-card bill. It would have been better if you had avoided that debt, but it does provide an opportunity for you to get a very high return by starting a savings program. Every dollar you save to pay down a credit-card debt effectively earns an interest rate of 18 percent, or whatever you are paying on the debt.

Look at it this way. If you put a dollar in an investment that is paying 18 percent, then one year from now it has added $1.18 to your net worth. If you save a dollar to pay off your credit-card debt, then one year from now it has also added $1.18 to your net worth. Your debt will be that much lower—first, from the dollar you saved that reduced your debt initially and, second, from the 18 cents you would have otherwise owed in interest.

Even if your credit-card rate is less than 18 percent, it is still much higher than what you will consistently earn on any other savings program you will ever have, unless you are extraordinarily lucky or good at investing. Of course you may not feel as though your savings are really earning 18 percent, since the money isn't actually being paid into your investment accounts. But it amounts to the same thing. The very first thing anyone who has a credit-card debt and is serious about achieving financial success should do is *pay that debt off,* from savings if necessary.

What if you do not have the funds to pay off your credit-card bill? Then take out a bank loan—the interest rate will be lower than your credit-card rate—and develop a plan to pay off the loan as quickly as possible, over the next six months, for example. Of course, you also need to make sure that you do not run up any other credit-card debt.

In addition to avoiding credit-card debt or paying it off immediately, a second way to stretch your money is to buy used items when they will serve you almost as well as new ones. The problem with buying things new is that they depreciate or decline in value almost immediately. Thus, while new items can be purchased, they cannot be owned as new items for long. Almost as soon as an item is purchased, it becomes "used" in terms of market value.

Buying things that are used—or, in today's parlance, preowned—can reap substantial savings. Consider the cost of purchasing a new automobile compared with a used one. For example, if you buy a brand-new Toyota Camry, which will cost you about $28,000, and trade it in after one year, you will receive about $18,000, or $10,000 less than you paid for it. If you drove the car 15,000 miles, then your depreciation cost—the cost to you of the decline in the car's value—is 66 cents per mile.

But instead of buying a new Camry, you can buy one that is a year old from a dealer. You will pay about $20,000. This is $8,000 less than it cost new (and about $2,000 more than the original owner received from the dealer).

Given how long cars last if you take care of them, you should easily be able to get excellent service from your used Camry for eight years, at which time you can probably sell it for about $2,000. Assuming that you drove 15,000 miles per year, your depreciation cost per mile will be $18,000/ 120,000 miles, or just 15 cents. This is 51 cents per mile less than the cost of driving a new car every year. Staying with the assumption that you drive 15,000 miles a year, the depreciation saving from the used car is $7,650 every year. Of course your repair bills may be somewhat higher after the car is a few years old, but even if they average $1,650 a year (very doubtful), you will still save $6,000 each year by sacrificing that new car smell.

Many other items are just as functional used as new and often much less expensive. Furniture, appliances (for example, refrigerators, washers, and dryers), and children's clothes and toys (which they outgrow and tire of quickly) come immediately to mind. We are not suggesting that you spend a lot of time at garage sales and used car lots. Given the value of your time, in many cases it will be more economical for you to purchase a product new rather than used, particularly if you plan to keep the item a long time. Instead, we are encouraging you to consider the potential savings that can often be derived from used purchases without your having to give up much in terms of consumer satisfaction. Do not pass up these opportunities to get more value from your money.

6. Begin Paying Into a "Real-World" Savings Account Every Month.

We have talked about the value of saving for your future. But you also need a real-world savings account. What is that? The real world has an endless string of surprise occurrences: the car breaks down, the roof leaks, you have a plumbing problem, your child breaks his arm—just to name a few.[3] We can't predict which ones will occur, or when. But we can predict that over any long period of time, each household will confront such costly items. Thus, it makes sense to plan for them. This is what your real-world savings account is for. It will help you deal with unexpected bills that could otherwise put you under severe emotional stress and into a financial bind.

The alternative is to wait until the surprise events occur and then try to devise a plan to deal with them. This will generally mean running up credit-card balances or some other method of borrowing funds on highly unfavorable terms. Then you have to figure out how you're going to cover the interest charges and eventually repay the funds. All of this leads to anxiety that is likely to result in unwise financial decisions.

How much should you set aside regularly to deal with such events? One approach would be to make a list of the various surprises of the past year and estimate how much each one cost you. Add the costs up, divide that number by twelve, and begin channeling that amount monthly into your real-world savings account. You might even want to pay a little more into the account just in case you confront higher future spending in this area. After all, if you pay too much into the account, you can build up a little cushion. If the funds in the account continue to grow, eventually you can use some of them for other purposes or allocate them into your retirement savings program. The key point is to consider the monthly allocations into your real-world savings account as a mandatory rather than an optional budget item. Thus they should be treated just like your mortgage payment, electric bill, and other regular expenditures.

A real-world savings account allows you to purchase a little peace of mind rather than worrying about the financial bumps of life. With such an account, you will be able to deal confidently with expenditures that, while unpredictable as to timing, can nonetheless be anticipated with a fair degree of accuracy. During periods when your surprise expenditures are below average, the balance in your real-world savings account will grow. When the surprise expenditures are atypically large, the funds in your account will be drawn down, but you can remain calm because you are prepared. This is an important element of what it means for you to take charge of your money rather than allowing money to take charge of you.

7. Put the Power of Compound Interest to Work for You.

In Element 3 we emphasized the importance of budgeting regularly, saving habitually, and spending your money effectively. There are two major reasons for starting now. First, as we discussed, those who yield to the many excuses not to start budgeting, saving, and spending wisely now will have a hard time doing so later. But in this element we want to talk more about the second reason to begin saving right away: the big payoff that comes from starting early.

A small head start in your savings program leads to a substantial increase in the payoff. Recall the example in Element 3 of the additional retirement wealth a young person could have by saving a modest amount from age twenty-two to thirty? Giving up just a little over $6,000 in purchasing power (assuming that the savings is taken from before-tax income) for those eight years can easily add over $153,000 to retirement wealth at age sixty-seven. The key to converting a small amount of money now into a large amount later is to start saving immediately to take full advantage of the "miracle of compound interest."

Compound interest is not really a miracle, but sometimes it seems that way. Despite the fact that it is easy to explain how compound interest works, the results are truly amazing. Compound interest is simply earning interest on interest. If you don't spend the interest earned on your savings this year, the interest will add to both your savings and the interest earned next year. By doing the same thing the next year, you then earn interest on your interest on your interest, etc. This may not seem like much, and for the first few years it doesn't add that much to your wealth. But before too long your wealth begins growing noticeably, and the larger it becomes, the faster it grows. It's like a small snowball rolling down a snow-covered mountain. At first it increases in size slowly. But each little bit of extra snow adds to the size, which allows even more snow to be accumulated, and soon it is huge, growing rapidly, and coming right at you.

The importance of starting your savings program early is explained by the gradual effect that compound interest has early on as it sets the stage for its accelerating effect later. The savings you make right before retirement won't add much more to your retirement wealth than the amount you save—a little but not much. The snowball that starts near the bottom of the mountain won't be much bigger when it stops rolling. So the sooner you start saving, the more time that early savings will have to grow, and the more dramatic the growth will be.

Consider a simple example. Assume a sixteen-year-old is deciding whether to start smoking. This is an important choice for several reasons, health considerations being the most important. However, in addition to the health factor, there is a financial reason for not smoking. The price of cigarettes is around $3.75 a pack in most states. So if our teenager—let's call him Roger—decides against smoking, he will save $1,370 a year (assuming he would have smoked a pack a day). Suppose that instead of spending this amount on something else, Roger invests it in a mutual fund that provides an annual rate of return of 7 percent a year in real terms—that is, after accounting for inflation. (Note: This 7 percent return is right at the annual rate of return of the Standard & Poor's (S&P) Index of the five hundred largest U.S. firms since 1926.) As Exhibit 10 illustrates, if Roger keeps this up for ten years, when he is twenty-six he will have accumulated $18,929 from savings of $13,700. Not bad for a rather small sacrifice—one that is, in fact, good for Roger.

But this is just liftoff; the payoff from compound interest is just getting started. If Roger keeps this savings plan going until he is thirty-six, he will have $56,164 from savings of $27,400. Continuing until he is forty-six will find him with $129,411 from savings of $41,100. And now the afterburners really start kicking in. By the time Roger is fifty-six he will have $273,500 from saving contributions of $54,800. As Exhibit 10 shows, when he retires at age sixty-seven he will have $597,301 from direct contributions of only $69,870. Thus, by choosing not to smoke, Roger accumulates almost $600,000 in retirement benefits—and this figure is in dollars with today's purchasing power![4]

Alternatively, consider what would happen if Roger smoked from age sixteen to twenty-six, then stopped smoking and started saving the price of a pack of cigarettes every day. It is good that he stopped smoking, and

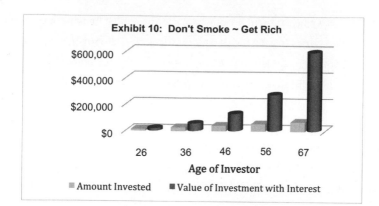

Source: Author's calculations. Assumes 7 percent interest per year.

he will still benefit from the savings. But by postponing his savings program by ten years, instead of having $597,301 at age sixty-seven, Roger will have only $294,015. Delaying a fifty-one-year saving program by ten years costs Roger $303,286 at retirement!

On the other hand, by saving just a little longer, you can derive benefits from the accelerating growth provided by compound interest. For example, Roger will have almost $700,000 in today's purchasing power if, after starting at sixteen, he keeps saving for just a little over two more years and retires a little after his sixty-ninth birthday. And the more you save, the more compound interest will boost your wealth. If Roger makes a few other rather minor sacrifices, such as buying used rather than new cars, eating a little less junk food from the vending machines, and not buying those lottery tickets (a person is far more likely to be hit by lightning than to win a lottery jackpot), he could easily have an additional million or more at retirement.

Again, our point is not that you should live a miserable life of austerity and sacrifice so that you can be rich when you retire. Where's the advantage in becoming rich in the future by living in poverty until the future arrives? Instead, we are stressing that ordinary people can have a high standard of living and still accumulate a lot of wealth because it does not take much savings to get a big payoff. Of the $597,301 Roger accumulated by not smoking, only $69,870 came from reducing his consumption. Indeed, people who save and invest will be able to consume far more than those who do not. At retirement—or sooner—Roger can start spending his wealth and end up having much more than if he had never saved.

All it takes is an early savings program, a little patience, knowing how to get a reasonable return on your savings (see the next two elements), and taking advantage of the power of compound interest.

8. Diversify—Don't Put All Your Eggs in One Basket.

Investments involve risk. The market value of a real estate or corporate stock investment can change dramatically in a relatively short period of time. Even if the nominal return is guaranteed, as in the case of high-quality bonds, changes in the interest and inflation rates can substantially change the value of the asset. If you have most of your wealth tied up in the ownership of a piece of real estate or a small number of corporate stocks (or even worse, a single stock), you are especially vulnerable. The recent experiences of those holding a large share of their assets in the equities of firms such as Enron, Bear Stearns and General Motors illustrate this point.

You can reduce your risk through diversification—holding a large number of unrelated assets. Diversification puts the law of large numbers to work for you. While some of the investments in a diversified portfolio will do poorly, others will do extremely well. The performance of the latter will offset that of the former, and the rate of return will converge toward the average.

For most people a home purchase is likely to be their major investment, at least initially. Buying a home you can afford, in an attractive community, and keeping it well-maintained can be a good investment. But, as the recent housing crisis illustrates, there are pitfalls to be avoided. You can avoid the worst problems by doing three things. First, do not buy a house until you are able to save enough for a 20 percent down payment. If your down payment is less than 20 percent, you will be vulnerable to housing price changes and your monthly housing payment will be higher because you will have to purchase costly mortgage insurance. Second, do not use a mortgage with a low teaser interest rate to purchase your home. These rates are often followed by sharply escalating interest rates, which will substantially increase your monthly mortgage payment. Third, as you build up equity in your house, do not take out another mortgage or borrow against your equity in order to increase your current consumption. Housing prices go down as well as up. Thus, safety dictates that it is important to maintain a sizable equity in your home. Living by these rules will encourage you to live within your means, and to economize on housing, as well as other expenditures.

Beyond investment in a home, for those seeking to build wealth without having to become involved in day-to-day business decision making, the stock market can provide attractive returns. It has done so historically. During the last two centuries, after adjustment for inflation, corporate stocks yielded a real rate of return of approximately 7 percent per year, compared to a real rate of return of about 3 percent for bonds.[5]

The risk with stocks is that no one can ever be sure what they will be worth at any specified time in the future; inevitably there will be periods over which the market value of your investments is falling, only to rise months or years later. But that risk, known as volatility, is a big reason why stocks yield a significantly higher rate of return than saving accounts, money market certificates, and short-term government bonds, all of which guarantee you a given amount in the future. Since most people value the additional certainty in the yields that bonds and savings accounts provide over stocks, the average return on stocks has to be higher to attract investors away from their less risky counterparts with more predictable returns.

The risks of stock market investments are substantially reduced if one continually adds to or holds a diverse portfolio of stocks over a lengthy period of time, say thirty or thirty-five years. Even a small investor can choose this option through an equity mutual fund, a corporation that buys and holds shares of stock in many firms. Historically, when a diverse set of stocks has been held over a lengthy time frame, the rate of return has been high and the variation in that return has been relatively small.

Diversification will reduce the volatility of investments in the stock market in two ways. When some firms do poorly, others do well. An oil price decline that causes lower profits in the oil industry will tend to boost profits in the airline industry because the cost of airline fuel will decline. When profits in the steel industry fall because steel prices decline, the lower steel prices will tend to boost the profits in the automobile industry. Of course general economic conditions can change, such as with a recession or an expansion, causing changes in the value of the stocks of almost all firms. But even in this case, diversification reduces the volatility in the value of your investments because a recession is worse for some firms and industries than others and a boom is better for some than for others. For example, the recession that harms Neiman Marcus may boost sales and profits for Walmart, at least relative to most firms.

Some employers offer retirement programs (such as a 401(k) plan) that will match your purchases of the company stock (but not investments in other firms) or will allow you to purchase the company stock at a substantial discount. Such a plan makes purchasing the stock of your company attractive. If you have substantial confidence in the company, you may want to take advantage of this offer. After a holding period, typically three years, these plans will permit you to sell the purchased shares and use the proceeds to undertake other investments. As soon as you are permitted to do so, you should choose this option. Failure to do so will mean that you will soon have too many of your investment eggs in the basket of the company for which you work. This places you in a position

of double jeopardy: Both your employment and the value of your investments depend substantially on the success of your employer. *Do not put
yourself in this position.*

We can summarize the importance of stock investments and diversity
this way: To achieve their financial potential, individuals must channel
their savings into investments that yield attractive returns. In the past,
long-term investments in the stock market have yielded high returns.
Stock mutual funds open possibilities for even small investors to hold a
diverse portfolio, add to it monthly, and still keep transaction costs low.
Investing in a diverse portfolio of stocks over a lengthy period of time
reduces the risk of stock ownership to a low level. All investments have
some uncertainty. But if the past century and a half are any guide, we can
confidently expect that over the long haul, a diverse portfolio of corporate stocks will yield a higher real return than will savings accounts,
bonds, certificates of deposit, money market funds, and similar financial
devices. Ownership of stock through mutual funds is particularly attractive for young people saving for their retirement years.

9. Indexed Equity Funds Can Help You Beat the Experts Without Taking Excessive Risk.

Many Americans refrain from investments in stocks because they feel
they do not have either the time or expertise to identify businesses that
are likely to be successful in the future. They are correct about the difficulties involved in forecasting the future direction of either individual
stocks or stock prices generally. No one can say for sure what will happen
to either the general level of stock prices or the prices of any specific
stock in the future.

Most economists accept the random walk theory. According to this
theory, current stock prices reflect the best information that is known
about the future state of corporate earnings, the health of the economy,
and other factors that influence stock prices. Therefore the future direction

of stock prices will be driven by surprise occurrences, things that people do not currently anticipate. By their very nature, these factors are unpredictable. If they were predictable, they would already be reflected in current stock prices.

Why not pick just the stocks that will do well, as Apple, Google and Microsoft have, and stay away from everything else? That is a great idea, except for one problem: The random walk theory also applies to the prices of specific stocks. The prices of stocks with attractive future profit potential will already reflect these prospects. The future price of a specific stock will be driven by unforeseen changes, and additional information about the prospects of the firm that will become known only with the passage of time. Countless factors affect the future price of a particular stock, and they are constantly changing in unpredictable ways. The price of Microsoft stock could be driven down, for example, because of an idea a high-school kid is working on in his basement right now. Thus there is no way that you can know ahead of time which stocks are going to rocket into the financial stratosphere and which ones are going to fizzle on the launch pad or crash after takeoff.

You may be able to improve your chances a little by studying the stock market, the details of particular corporations, and economic trends and forecasts. For most of us, however, the best option will be to channel our long-term (that is, retirement) savings into a stock index mutual fund. An index fund is a special type of mutual fund. An index fund holds stocks in the same proportion as their representation in broad indexes of the stock market, such as the S&P 500 or the Dow Jones Industrials. Very little trading is necessary to maintain a portfolio of stocks that mirrors a broad index. Neither is it necessary for index funds to undertake research evaluating the future prospects of companies. Because of these two factors, the operating costs of index funds are substantially lower, usually 1 or 2 percentage points lower, than those of managed funds. As

a result, index funds charge lower fees and therefore a larger share of your investment flows directly into the purchase of stock.

A mutual fund that is indexed to a broad stock market indicator such as the S&P 500 will earn approximately the average stock market return for its shareholders. What is so great about the average return? As we noted earlier, historically the stock market has yielded an average real rate of return of about 7 percent. That means that the real value, the value adjusted for inflation, of your stock holdings doubles approximately every ten years. That's not bad. Even more important, the average rate of return yielded by a broad index fund beats the return of almost all managed mutual funds when comparisons are made over periods of time such as a decade. Over the typical ten-year period, the S&P 500 has yielded a higher return than 85 percent of the actively managed funds. Over twenty-year periods, mutual funds indexed to the S&P 500 have generally outperformed about 98 percent of the actively managed funds.[6] Thus the odds are very low, about one in fifty, that you or anyone else will be able to select an actively managed fund that will do better than the market average *over the long run.*

Just because a managed mutual fund does well for a few years or even a decade, it does not follow that it will do well in the future. For example, the top twenty managed equity funds during the 1980s outperformed the S&P 500 Index by 3.9 percent per year over the decade. But if investors entering the market in 1990 thought they would beat the market by choosing the hot funds of the 1980s, they would have been disappointed. The top twenty funds of the 1980s underperformed the S&P Index by 1.2 percent per year during the 1990s.

The hot funds during the stock market bubble of the late 1990s were an even more misleading investment indicator. Over the two-year period 1998–99 the top-performing managed fund was Van Wagoner Emerging Growth, with a 105.52 percent average annual return. But over the two-year period 2000–2001, this fund ranked 1,106 with an average annual return of *minus* 43.54 percent.[7]

The most important thing to take from this element is: Do not allow a lack of time and expertise to keep you out of equity investments. You do not have to do a lot of research or be a "super stock picker" in order to be highly successful as an investor. The stock market has historically yielded higher returns than other major investment categories, and index funds make it possible for the ordinary investor to earn these returns without worrying about trying to pick either individual stocks or a specific mutual fund. Of course there will be ups and downs and even some fairly lengthy periods of declining stock prices. Therefore many investors will want to reduce equities as a percentage of their asset holdings as they approach retirement (see the following element). But based on a lengthy history of stock market performance, the long-term yield derived from a broad index of the stock market can be expected to exceed that of any other alternative, including managed equity funds.[8]

10. Invest in Stocks for Long-Run Objectives, but As the Need for Money Approaches, Increase the Proportion of Bonds.

As we previously mentioned, when held over a lengthy time period, a diverse holding of stocks has historically yielded both a high and a relatively stable rate of return. Exhibit 11 illustrates this point. This exhibit provides data for the highest and lowest average annual real rate of return (the return adjusted for inflation) earned from broad stock market investments for periods of varying length between the years 1871 and 2009. The exhibit assumes that the investor paid a fixed amount annually into a mutual fund that mirrored the Standard & Poor's 500 Index, a basket of stocks that represents the broad stock market.[9] Clearly, huge swings are possible when stocks are held for only a short time period. During the 1871–2009 period, the single-year returns of the S&P 500 ranged from 47.2 percent

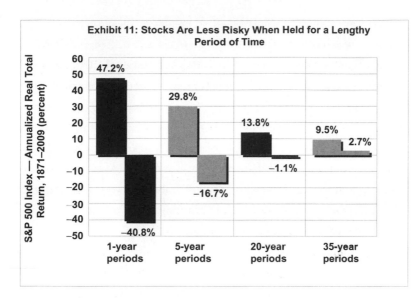

Exhibit 11: Stocks Are Less Risky When Held for a Lengthy Period of Time

Source: Liqun Liu, Andrew J. Rettenmaier, and Zijun Wang, "Social Security and Market Risk," National Center for Policy Analysis Working Paper Number 244 (July 2001). The returns are based on the assumption that an individual invests a xed amount for each year in the investment period. Data are updated through 2008.

to −40.8 percent. Even over a five-year period, the compound annual returns ranged from 29.8 percent to −16.7 percent.

However, note how the "best returns" and "worst returns" converge as the length of the investment period increases. When a thirty-five-year period is considered, the compound annual return for the best thirty-five years between 1871 and 2009 was 9.5 percent, compared to 2.7 percent for the worst thirty-five years. Thus, the annual real return of stocks during the worst-case scenario was about the same as the real return for bonds. This high and relatively stable return, when held over a lengthy time period, makes stocks particularly attractive when saving long-term for retirement.

When saving for retirement, it is also important to take advantage of one or more of the several retirement saving plans that provide favorable tax treatment. We recommend that you speak with a competent tax adviser to determine which plan is best for you. The main features, however, are seen in three plans—401(k) plans, or the equivalent 403(b) plans for teachers; traditional Individual Retirement Accounts (IRAs); and Roth IRAs. When investing in 401(k) or traditional IRAs your contributions are deductible from your taxable income, so your take-home income is reduced by less than the amount you are saving. You have to pay taxes on your accumulated savings eventually, but not until you retire, when you may be in a lower income-tax bracket. With Roth IRAs, your contributions are not deductable from your taxable income, so your take-home income is reduced by the full amount of your contributions into your plan, but your retirement withdrawals are not taxable. Thus, the value of your investments grow tax-free in Roth IRAs. Under certain conditions this deferred tax break can more than make up for the fact that you will probably save less with a Roth than with a traditional IRA. For example, a Roth IRA will probably be better for you if you believe your tax rate is lower now than it will be when you retire. But other factors can be important also, which is why you should get some impartial and expert advice before making a decision.

While the long-term return of stocks is approximately twice that of bonds, the latter will yield a more stable return over shorter time periods. The greatest risk of owning bonds is inflation, which lessens the value of both the principal and the fixed-interest payments. However, that risk can be reduced or eliminated with the use of TIPS, or Treasury Inflation-Protected Securities. This product is a form of a U.S. Treasury bond that was first sold in 1997. TIPS return the principal, a fixed-interest rate that depends on the market rate when they are purchased, and an additional payment to adjust for inflation. Because unanticipated inflation is what makes bond payments worth less than expected, buying and holding TIPS will protect the holder against that risk. TIPS are particularly attractive for retirees seeking to generate a specific stream of real purchasing power from their assets.

An additional risk associated with bonds is the impact of changes in interest rates. Assume that you buy a $1,000, thirty-year bond that pays 5 percent interest. This bond promises to pay you $50 in interest every year for thirty years, at which time it matures and you get $1,000. But if the overall or general interest rate increases to 10 percent soon after you buy this bond, then your bond will immediately fall in value to about half of what you paid for it. At a 10 percent interest rate, an investor can get $50 in interest every year by buying a $500 bond. So $500 is about all anyone will be willing to pay for your $1,000 bond. Of course if the interest rate drops to 2.5 percent soon after you buy your thirty-year, 5 percent bond, then its price will approximately *double* in value. But this is more volatility (or risk) than you want to take if you are saving for something you expect to buy in five years.

Given a five-year horizon, it is much safer to buy a bond that matures in five years, at which point you receive all of your $1,000 back. As a general proposition, when buying bonds you should buy those that mature at about the time you expect to need the funds, since you get the face amount of the bond back at maturity no matter what the interest rate is at the time. Because large changes in interest rates are usually the result of changes in inflation, TIPS protect against much of the risk associated with interest-rate changes.

How long should a portfolio consist of stocks, and when should the move to bonds be made? That depends on the length of time for the investment. Relatively short-term investments may do best in bonds exclusively. For example, a young couple saving to place 20 percent down to buy a house may be better off avoiding the stock market entirely—for that portion of their savings *only*—and investing it in bonds. That is because purchasing a house or condominium often involves saving for just a few years. In contrast, a couple might save for eighteen years to finance a college education for a newborn or for thirty-five to forty-five years to build up savings for their retirement. In these two cases, equities should be an important part of, or perhaps the entire, investment fund for most of the saving years.

The parents of a newborn who begin saving right away for the child's college education have more years to build wealth and to diversify the risk of capitalizing on stocks to build it faster as well. In that case, having some of that college portfolio in equities may make sense. The Great Recession of recent years, however, has shown that even with an 18-year horizon, some parents may wish they had taken a more cautious path, despite the lower expected returns. Again, investors seeking to reduce risk in their college funds can do so by holding fewer stocks and more bonds, especially TIPS, which are likely to fluctuate far less in value over a few years' time.

As people earn more and live longer, saving for retirement expenses becomes ever more important. We don't want to drastically, and negatively, alter our lifestyle upon retirement; and we cannot afford to outlive our retirement nest eggs. For the saver whose retirement is more than ten years ahead, a diversified portfolio of stocks, such as a mutual fund indexed to the S&P 500, probably makes the best investment portfolio. For the more conservative saver, having 10, 20, or even 40 percent of one's portfolio in bonds will offer some peace of mind, even though total returns will probably be lower in the end. The value of bond holdings will not fluctuate as much, month by month or year by year.

As the need for retirement income approaches, it is prudent for all but the most wealthy among us to begin to switch an all-stock portfolio gradually into bonds. When that switch should begin depends partly on when and how much money is needed. For those individuals with a large portfolio or a good pension income relative to their retirement income needs, much of their savings can be left longer in equities to maximize expected total return. The goal of switching to bonds is primarily to avoid the *need* to sell stocks at temporarily low stock prices. The more frequently you turn to your portfolio to meet monthly living expenses, the more important it is to reduce risk by moving strategically and gradually into bonds. Once again TIPS may well be a good choice. In any case, buying bonds that mature as the funds are needed provides a method of locking in a known return until you expect to use the funds.

Our advice to those seeking to prepare for future retirement can be summed up this way: Start saving for retirement early; take advantage of 401(k) plans, Individual Retirement Accounts (IRAs) and other tax breaks; and stay with diversified portfolios of stocks until the need for funds is near enough in time to justify gradual shifts toward lower-risk, lower-return assets such as bonds.

11. Beware of Investment Schemes Promising High Returns with Little or No Risk.

Whenever you are offered what seems to be an extremely attractive business proposition, it pays to be skeptical. Put yourself in the position of the person offering the deal. Anyone who is looking for money to finance a project will turn first to low-cost sources and methods of finance. A low-risk proposition with a high return is easy to sell to bank lenders and other investment specialists who offer investment funding at normal rates of interest. Finding individual investors and offering them a high rate of return makes no sense if low-cost financing is available. If it is not, then the project is almost certainly higher risk than normal sources of business finance will accept. Should you accept that risk? At the very least, you should recognize that it is not a low-risk proposition. Count on it: high potential returns on investment inevitably come with high risk; that is, they are dangerous. If banks and professional investors are not interested in the investment, you should ask yourself, "Why should I be?"

Further, there is the issue of investor vulnerability. Investors are subject to what economists call the principal-agent problem. This problem arises when there is a potential conflict between what is best for the principal (in this case the investor or owner of funds) and what is best for an agent who is paid to do something on behalf of the principal. If you have ever taken a malfunctioning automobile to a mechanic for repair services, you have some experience with this potential conflict. As the mechanic reviews your situation, you, the principal, are hoping that he or she will be a good agent for you and tell you that the problem is minor and that it can be fixed quickly and economically. The mechanic, however, may prefer that you have a really serious problem that will lead to substantial income from selling parts and labor to fix your car. Because the mechanic is likely to know more about automobiles, you are in a vulnerable position.

Similarly, when undertaking an investment, you, as the principal, are vulnerable. The interests of those marketing the investment to you are almost always far different than yours. While you want to earn an attractive return, they are likely to be primarily interested in the commission on the sale or earnings derived from management fees or a high salary related to the business venture. Put bluntly, their primary interest is served by getting their hands on your money. They do not necessarily seek to defraud you; they may well believe that the investment is a genuine opportunity with substantial earning potential. But no matter how nice they are, how well you know them, or how much it appears that they want to help you, their interests are different from yours. Moreover, once they have your money, you will be in a weak position to alter the situation. Thus you need to recognize both the potential conflict and the vulnerability of your position, and act accordingly.

How can you tell beforehand whether an investment is a wise one? There is no "silver bullet" that can assure positive results from all investment decisions. But there are things you can do that will help you avoid investment disasters costing you tens of thousands of dollars. The following six guidelines are particularly important.

If it looks too good to be true, it probably is. This is an old cliché, but it is nonetheless true. Some investment marketers may be willing to do just about anything to obtain your money because once they do, they are in charge and you are vulnerable.

Deal only with parties that have a reputation to protect. Established companies with a good reputation will be reluctant to direct their clients into risky investments. For example, an initial public stock offering by an upstart brokerage firm with which only a few are familiar is far more likely to result in disaster than the offering of an established firm with a substantial reputation on the line.

Never purchase an investment solicited by telephone or e-mail. Such marketing is a technique used by those looking for suckers. Do not be one.

Do not allow yourself to be forced into a quick decision. Take time to develop an investment strategy and do not be pressured into a hasty decision.

Do not allow friendship to influence an investment decision. Numerous people have been directed into bad investments by their friends. If you want to keep a person as your friend, invest your money somewhere else.

If high-pressure marketing is involved, grab your checkbook and run. Attractive investments can be sold without the use of high-pressure marketing techniques. If you already have a substantial portfolio, there may be a place in it for high-risk investments, including "junk bonds" and precious metals. But those investments must come from funds that you can afford to lose. If you are looking for a sound way to build wealth, most of your funds should be in more mundane lower-risk investments.

12. Teach Your Children How to Earn Money and Spend It Wisely.

So far we have been discussing how you can become wealthy as you move toward retirement by following some simple rules with a measure of patience and persistence. In this element we shift the focus from you to your children, or your future children.

Parents want their children to be successful, not just financially, but in all aspects of life. General well-being and financial success tend to go together, and the connection is not accidental. Those who develop the habits of working diligently, setting goals and achieving them, and avoiding the temptations of instant gratification by considering the future consequences of current choices are typically more successful in all walks of life than those who don't. There are many ways to instill these attributes in your children. Getting them started on an earnings and savings program at an early age is one of them.

One of the most important ways to teach young people responsibility is by helping them understand that money is earned; it is not manna from heaven. Instead of just giving your children an allowance, pay them for performing certain tasks around the house and for achieving educational goals. Couple these payments with some discussion explaining that the money that you earn is a measure of how well you help others. Money is not just a means of getting more of what you want, it is also a measure of your contribution in helping others get more of what *they* want. The best way to earn more money is by coming up with better ways of making other people better off. This entrepreneurial lesson will pay important dividends during your children's careers, no matter what those careers turn out to be.

Of course you will buy your children many things without requiring that they earn the money for them. But even when you are paying for your children's purchases, it is possible to provide them with an understanding of the costs and trade-offs that are inherent in all expenditures. For example, all four of the authors have firsthand experience with the desires of teenagers to buy the most fashionable brand of clothing, even when cheaper brands are just as functional. Because we are economists, we often responded to the desires of our children in a similar manner. We gave them money to buy their preferred outfit, letting them know that it was their money, and if they bought a cheaper outfit they could keep the savings and use it for anything they wanted. Sometimes they bought the most expensive outfit, but sometimes they didn't. The important point is that they faced the cost of their purchasing decisions and reaped the benefits if they chose to economize. This is what consumer decision making in the real world is all about.

This strategy can also reduce conflict between parents and children. An incident from the Gwartney family history illustrates this point. As the Gwartneys and their four boys were traveling in the 1980s from Florida to Montana, a conflict arose at the first lunch stop. The Gwartneys' eleven-year-old son wanted to order a T-bone steak for lunch, but Dad thought a hamburger and fries were more suitable (and less than half the cost). After some discussion, Dad eventually won, but the eleven-year-old was not a happy traveler. The scene repeated itself at dinner, as the eleven-year-old, along with one of the older boys, wanted to order steak and lobster, whereas Dad was thinking of something far more economical. After only two meals the family faced a dilemma: either they were going to be decidedly poorer by the time they got to Montana or this was not going to be a pleasant trip.

While discussing the matter after dinner, Mom and Dad came up with a plan: They would give each of the boys an adequate, but not exorbitant, daily meal allowance. If the meal cost exceeded the allowance, the boy would have to make up the difference from funds he had saved for the purchase of souvenirs and similar items. But if meal expenditures were less than the allowance, each could pocket the difference. Recognizing that they would be able to eat quite well and still have funds left over for personal use, all of the boys were delighted with this arrangement. Wow! What an impact this had on decision making! The eleven-year-old quickly discovered the free Jell-O that was available at several restaurants, and he saved almost all of his allowance the first day. On the second day, he also saved a substantial amount by discovering how tasty soup could be. By the third day, he was ordering adequate but economical meals while still saving a bit from his daily allowance. The older boys followed a similar course, although their adjustments were not quite so dramatic. Most significant, there were no more conflicts over meals, the rest of the trip to Montana was a pleasant one, and they were still able to afford steak and lobster one evening.

Throughout their lives, all of our children will have to decide how they are going to spend a limited income. If they spend more on one item, they will have to spend less on others. We all have to make trade-offs. Beginning at an early age, we need to teach our children about this reality and provide them with experiences that will help them learn to choose wisely.

Dealing with the cost of a college education provides an excellent opportunity to teach your children important lessons in personal finance. There is certainly more than one way this issue can be handled. As we previously discussed, some families will want to begin a college savings program as soon as a child is born. This will provide an excellent opportunity to teach your children about the power of compound interest and the payoff from patience. As children grow and have more opportunity to earn, they should be encouraged to channel some of their earnings into the savings program. The program can be used to illustrate the benefits of starting early. Children can experience real excitement in understanding that the few dollars a week that are saved now can turn into tens of thousands of dollars when one is an adult. They can begin to see saving as an exhilarating game that builds a strong sense of responsibility and feeling of personal control over one's future. In fact, development of this attribute may be even more important than the funds set aside for college.

Some parents feel a responsibility to pay the full cost of a college education for their children. Relieving a child from the financial responsibilities of college can provide additional time and resources to take fuller advantage of the educational and social opportunities. But there are also dangers. Providing college-age children with a free ride can undermine personal responsibility. The authors, having spent their careers on college campuses, can assure you that a sizable share of college students are spending their parents' savings primarily on having a good time. For some the weekend starts on Thursday and runs through at least Monday evening. Classes can sometimes be a minor inconvenience, but as long as these students earn passing grades, or at least make their parents think they are, they can let the good times roll.

People spend their own money more wisely than they spend the money of others. College students are no exception to this rule. Thus we believe that college students will be more likely to benefit from the educational experience when they have some responsibility for the costs. One approach is to provide your children with ample earning opportunities beginning at an early age while at the same time informing them that you will match the funds they set aside for a college education as well as matching other funds they earn in the form of scholarships. In other words, you will pay half of the total expenditure, whether it is high or low. This will increase their incentive to earn, save, budget, and succeed in elementary and secondary school. It will also give them an incentive to both economize on the cost of college and strive to get the most out of their college years. This is the path chosen by one of the authors, and it worked out quite well.

To a large degree success in life is about setting goals, working hard to achieve them, figuring out how to make our services useful to others, saving for a specific purpose, and spending money wisely. Good parenting involves helping our children develop these attributes starting early in life. Doing so can be both challenging and fun. Who said economics is the "dismal science"?

Acknowledgments

The authors would like to thank the following individuals for helpful comments on earlier drafts of this book: Joab Corey, David Gwartney, Randall Holcombe, Robert Lawson, Ninos Malek, Tom Palmer, Russell Sobel, and Amy Willis. Joe Connors and Rosemary Fike helped with the preparation of the exhibits and provided other research assistance. Amy Gwartney edited the entire manuscript and made numerous modifications that improved both the readability and content. Jane Shaw Stroup and Cindy Crain-Lee also provided helpful comments on several sections of the book. We would also like to express our appreciation to Philip Revzin, senior editor at St. Martin's Press, for his handling of editorial responsibilities. We would also like to express our appreciation to the Earhart Foundation for financial support. Hundreds of teachers, and their students, benefited greatly from the workshops that this support made possible. Through the years, we have had numerous discussions, both in and out of class, with students who provided us with insightful comments and challenging questions that provided the foundation for this project. We cherish these interactions and dedicate the book to these students who have enriched our lives.

Notes

Part I: Twelve Key Elements of Economics

1. Philip K. Howard, *The Death of Common Sense* (New York: Random House, 1994): 3–5.
2. See the chapter "Time for Symphonies and Softball" in W. Michael Cox and Richard Alm, *Myths of Rich and Poor* (New York: Basic Books, 1999).
3. The website http://CommonSenseEconomics.com accompanies this book. It provides a supplementary unit on demand and supply, which analyzes the factors that shift the demand and supply curves and provides a more detailed explanation of how market prices adjust to various types of dynamic change. If you would like more depth on this topic, please see this supplementary unit on the CSE website.
4. Adam Smith, *An Inquiry into the Nature and Causes of the Wealth of Nations*, Volume II, Glasgow Edition (Indianapolis: Liberty Fund, Inc., [1776] 1981): 660. Also available at: http://www.econlib.org/library/Smith/smWN.html.
5. Ibid.: 454.
6. F. A. Hayek, "The Use of Knowledge in Society," *American Economic Review* 35 (September 1945): 519–30.
7. Henry Hazlitt, *Economics in One Lesson* (New Rochelle: Arlington House, 1979), 103.
8. Assar Lindbeck, *The Political Economy of the New Left* (New York: Harper & Row, 1972), 39.

Part II: Seven Major Sources of Economic Progress

1. The most widely used measure of total output is Gross Domestic Product (GDP). Changes in GDP are also widely used to measure the growth of an economy. For more information on GDP, see Supplementary Unit 3 "Gross Domestic Product (GDP): What Is It and How Is It Measured?" at the website accompanying this book: http://CommonSenseEconomics .com.

2. The leading contributors to the modern theory of growth presented here are Nobel laureate Douglass C. North and the late Peter Bauer. See P. T. Bauer, *Dissent on Development: Studies and Debates in Development Economics* (Cambridge: Harvard University Press, 1972); and D. C. North, *Institutions, Institutional Change, and Economic Performance* (Cambridge: Cambridge University Press, 1990).

3. Tom Bethell, *The Noblest Triumph* (New York: St. Martin's Press, 1998), 10.

4. For additional information, see John McMillan, *Reinventing the Bazaar: A Natural History of Markets* (New York: Norton, 2002), 94–101. As McMillan points out, real privatization would have been preferred. Nonetheless, the movement toward private ownership was still "the biggest anti-poverty program the world has ever seen." (See page 94.)

5. There have been many examples of animal species that humans have hunted to extinction. Passenger pigeons are an example. They were hunted for meat; whales were hunted mainly for oil. But pigeons were such a small part of the market for meat that even as they began to disappear, the price of meat did not increase enough to call forth either preservation efforts or a large-scale increase in the production of meats. There was no crisis. So their disappearance became complete. If whales had been intensively hunted only for their meat, and not mainly for oil, they also might have disappeared. But whale oil was so important in the market for light, that when its price rose sharply, a substitute was found that reduced the demand for whale oil and its price, saving the whales.

6. Clair Wilcox, *Competition and Monopoly in American Industry*. Monograph no. 21, Temporary National Economic Committee, Investigation of Concentration of Economic Power, 76th Cong. 3d sess. (Washington, D.C.: U.S. Government Printing Office, 1940).

7. Adam Smith, *An Inquiry into the Nature and Causes of the Wealth of Nations*, Volume I, Glasgow Edition (Indianapolis: Liberty Fund, Inc., [1776] 1981): 18. Also available at: http://www.econlib.org/library/Smith/smWN.html.

8. World Bank, *Doing Business 2009*. (Washington, D.C.)

9. For evidence on this point, see Edward Bierhanzl and James Gwartney, "Regulation, Unions, and Labor Markets," *Regulation* (Summer 1998): 40–53.

10. These figures are from the Center for Responsive Politics, "Lobbying: Top Spenders, 2008," available at http://www.opensecrets.org/lobby/top.php?indexType=s. (For additional details, see Peter J. Wallison and Charles W. Calomiris, "The Destruction of Fannie Mae and Freddie Mac," 2008, American Enterprise Institute, available at http://www.aei.org/outlook/28704.)

11. For a more comprehensive analysis of the Great Recession of 2008, see Supplementary Unit 7, "The Economic Crisis of 2008: Causes and Lessons for the Future" posted on the CSE website: http://Common SenseEconomics.com.

12. Supplementary Unit 2, "Consumer Price Index and Measurement of Inflation," and Unit 6, "Monetary Policy: How Is It Conducted and How Does It Affect the Economy?," are related to the focus of this element. These units provide additional details on inflation and money. Both units are available on the CSE website: http://CommonSenseEconomics.com.

13. For a comprehensive analysis of monetary policy and the Crisis of 2008, see John Taylor, *Getting Off Track: How Government Actions and Interventions Caused, Prolonged, and Worsened the Financial Crisis*. Stanford: Hoover Institution Press, 2009.

14. Stressing the historical relationship between monetary and economic instability, Friedman stated: "Every major contraction in this country has been either produced by monetary disorder or greatly exacerbated by monetary disorder. Every major inflation episode has been produced by monetary expansion." See Milton Friedman, "The Role of Monetary Policy," *American Economic Review* 58 (March 1968): 12.

15. For additional information on taxes and other dimensions of economic policy during the Great Depression era, see Supplementary Unit 8, "Lessons from the Great Depression," available on the CSE website http://CommonSenseEconomics.com.

16. Henry George, *Protection or Free Trade* (New York: Robert Schalkenbach Foundation, 1980).

17. Many of the "job savers" act as if foreigners are willing to supply us with goods without ever using their acquired dollars to purchase things from us. But this is not the case. If foreigners were willing to sell things to us for dollars and never use the dollars to buy products from us, it would be as though we could write checks for anything we wanted without anyone ever cashing them. Wouldn't that be great? In fact, however, people do cash our checks when we buy things from them. They don't actually want our checks; they want the things that money from our checking accounts can buy. Similarly, people in other countries who export products to us don't want our money; they want what the money can buy. Otherwise, we could just print the dollars we send them to get their goods as cheaply as possible, without fear of inflation, because the dollars would not come back to buy things in our market. But most of the dollars do come back in the form of foreign purchases. Thus, our purchases from foreigners—our imports—generate the demand for our exports.

18. When the exchange rate is determined by market forces, equilibrium in this market will bring the purchases of goods, services, and assets (including both real and financial assets such as bonds) from foreigners into balance with the sale of these items to foreigners. During the last couple of decades, U.S. imports of goods and services have persistently exceeded exports. With market-determined exchange rates, such trade deficits will be largely offset by an inflow of capital of similar magnitude. The capital inflow will result in lower interest rates, more investment, and additional employment. Thus, even in this case, there is no reason to anticipate that there will be a negative impact on employment. The U.S. experience illustrates this point. Even though trade deficits were present throughout most of the 1980–2005 period, employment in the United States expanded by more than 35 million.

19. The same logic applies to "outsourcing," undertaking certain activities abroad in order to reduce cost. If an activity can be handled at a lower cost abroad, doing so will release domestic resources that can be employed in higher productive activities. As a result, output will be larger and income levels higher.

20. An abridged version of Frédéric Bastiat's "Competition with the Sun" is available on the CSE website: http://CommonSenseEconomics.com.

21. As quoted in Frank Whitson Fetter, "Congressional Tariff Theory," *American Economic Review* 23 (September 1933): 413–27.

22. For additional information on the impact of the Smoot-Hawley legislation and other dimensions of economic policy during the Great Depression era, see Supplementary Unit 8, "Lessons from the Great Depression," available on the CSE website http://CommonSenseEconomics.com.

23. For additional details, see James Gwartney and Robert Lawson, *Economic Freedom of the World: 2009 Report* (Vancouver: Fraser Institute, 2009), and the website http://www.freetheworld.com.

24. Countries with lower initial income levels should grow more rapidly than those with higher incomes (holding other factors constant). After all, the low-income countries are in a position to adopt technologies and business practices that have proven successful in the higher-income countries. The freer economies have higher initial income levels, a fact that makes their more rapid growth all the more impressive. It should be noted, however, that the world's fastest growth rates have been registered by low-income countries after they achieved relatively good economic freedom ratings (for example, EFW ratings of 6.0 or better during 1980–2000). Thus, low-income countries can achieve highly impressive rates of economic growth when they adopt institutions and policies that are consistent with economic freedom.

25. See Joseph Connors and James Gwartney, "Economic Freedom and Global Poverty," in *Accepting the Invisible Hand*, ed. Mark D. White (New York: Palgrave Macmillan, forthcoming).

Part III: Economic Progress and the Role of Government

1. Thomas Jefferson, First Inaugural Address, March 4, 1801.

2. *The Collected Works of Abraham Lincoln*, edited by Roy P. Basler, V2 (Piscataway, N.J.: Rutgers University Press, 1953), 220.

3. W. Mark Crain and Thomas D. Hopkins, "The Impact of Regulatory Costs on Small Firms" (Washington, D.C.: U.S. Small Business Administration, 2001), p. 24. Available online at http://www.sba.gov/advo/research/rs207tot.pdf. The updated and extended report, by W. Mark Crain, "The Impact of Regulatory Costs on Small Firms" (Washington, D.C.: U.S. Small Business Administration, 2005), p. 4, also available online at http://www.sba.gov/advo/research/rs264tot.pdf.

4. Quotation is from the *Wall Street Journal,* December 16, 1983.

5. For additional details on the sugar program, see Aaron Lukas, "A Sticky State of Affairs: Sugar and the U.S.–Australia Free-Trade Agreement" (Washington, D.C.: Cato Institute, 2004). In recent years candy manufacturers and other major users of sugar have been moving to Canada, Mexico, and other countries where sugar can be purchased at the world market price. Illustrating our earlier discussion of trade, the import restrictions that "saved" jobs in the sugar-growing industry caused job losses in other industries, particularly those that use sugar intensely. It will be interesting to see if the increasing visibility of the job losses among candy manufacturers will weaken the political clout of the sugar growers.

6. James Buchanan, *The Deficit and American Democracy* (Memphis: P. K. Steidman Foundation, 1984).

7. We are indebted to E. C. Pasour Jr., longtime professor of economics at North Carolina State University, for this example.

8. James R. Schlesinger, "Systems Analysis and the Political Process," *Journal of Law & Economics* 11, no. 2 (October 1968): 281.

9. See James Gwartney and Richard Stroup, "Transfers, Equality, and the Limits of Public Policy," *Cato Journal* (Spring/Summer 1986), for a detailed analysis of this issue.

10. See Chris Edwards, "Federal Subsidy Programs Top 2000" (Washington, D.C.: Cato Institute, 2010). Also available online at http://www.cato-at-liberty.org/2010/01/25/federal-subsidy-programs-top-2000.

11. Others attribute this statement to Lord Thomas Macaulay. The author cannot be verified with certainty. For additional information on this topic, see Loren Collins, "The Truth About Tytler" at: http://www.lorencollins.net/tytler.html.

12. James Gwartney and Richard Stroup, op. cit.

13. Fred A. Shannon, "The Homestead Act and the Labor Surplus," *American Historical Review* 41 (July 1936): 637–651.

14. For evidence on this point, see Lawrence Katz and Bruce Meyer, "The Impact of the Potential Duration of Unemployment Benefits on the Duration of Unemployment," *Journal of Public Economics* 41, no. 1 (February 1990): 45–72.

15. Ron Haskins and Isabel V. Sawhill, *Opportunity Society* (Washington, D.C.: Brookings Institution Press, 2009).

16. Adam Smith, *The Theory of Moral Sentiments,* Glasgow Edition of Oxford University Press (Indianapolis: Liberty Fund, Inc., [1790] 1976): 233-34. Also available at: http://www.econlib.org/library/Smith/smMS6 .html#VI.II.42).

17. Arthur Laffer and Stephen Moore, "Soak the Rich, Lose the Rich; Americans Know How to Use the Moving Van to Escape High Taxes," *Wall Street Journal,* May 18, 2009.

18. Walter Lippmann, *The Good Society* (New York: Grosset & Dunlap, 1956), 38.

19. Points (b) and (c) are borrowed from Milton and Rose Friedman, *Free to Choose* (New York: Harcourt Brace Jovanovich, 1980). See particularly chapter 10.

20. It is important to distinguish between licensing and certification. Licensing requirements prohibit the practice of an occupation or profession without the permission of the state. They are a clear restraint on trade. In contrast, certification merely requires one to supply customers with information (for example, tests passed or educational levels achieved). As long as they were merely informational, certification requirements would not be prohibited by this amendment.

21. The federal government levies payroll, excise, and corporate taxes as well as the personal income tax. But the payroll tax is directed toward only two programs: Social Security and Medicare. Moreover, the benefits promised to Social Security recipients are related to the federal payroll taxes received. The personal income tax provides the bulk of federal revenue and it is the driving force underlying subsidies, special-interest spending, and the politicization of the economy. These factors, along with the ease with which the voting procedure can be integrated with the collection of the tax, explain why it makes sense to limit the voting on the budget constraint to those paying federal personal income tax.

22. It is very difficult to design rules that will prevent politicians from trading government favors for political contributions and other forms of special interest support. Groups interested in restricting such activities might request candidates to sign a statement promising they would not do things like (1) vote for subsidies and tax breaks that favor some businesses and regions relative to others, (2) place earmarks in legislation, (3) vote for any legislation with earmarks, or (4) accept contributions from the owners,

high level management or political action committees of any business or organization with sizable government contracts or grants. Of course, candidates would not have to sign pledges like these, but doing so might provide them with a competitive advantage, and if they signed the pledge and later broke it, this would tend to erode their credibility. There is some evidence that pledges like these exert an impact. For example, candidates running for office in New Hampshire have found it useful to sign a promise opposing a personal income tax, and these promises have generally been kept.

Part IV: *Twelve Elements of Practical Personal Finance*

1. Thomas Stanley and William D. Danko point out in their best seller, *The Millionaire Next Door* (Atlanta: Longstreet Press, 1996), that the most common characteristic of millionaires is that they have lived beneath their means for a long time. Over half of them never received any inheritance and fewer than 20 percent received 10 percent or more of their wealth from inheritance (p. 16).

2. Some may need creative methods of controlling impulse purchases with a credit card. If this is the case, economist and financial adviser William C. Wood suggests that you freeze your credit card inside a block of ice in your refrigerator. By the time the ice thaws, your impulse to buy may have cooled. For an excellent book on personal finance written from a Christian perspective, see William C. Wood, *Getting a Grip on Your Money* (Downers Grove, IL: Inter-Varsity Press, 2002).

3. Prof. William C. Wood calls such items "SIT expenditures." Wood indicates that "SIT stands for two things: (1) sit down when you get an unexpected bill, and (2) surprises, insurance and taxes."

4. Our calculations assume that your investments yield a return of 7 percent every year. Obviously this is unlikely to happen. Even though you can expect an average annual return of approximately 7 percent, this return will vary from year to year. This can make a difference in how much you accumulate at retirement, but the difference is likely to be small.

5. A 7 percent real rate of return may not sound like much compared to what some stocks, such as Dell and Microsoft, have yielded. But a 7 percent compounded rate of return means that the value of your savings will dou-

ble every ten years. In contrast, it will take thirty-five years to double your money at a 2 percent interest rate, the approximate after-tax return earned historically by savings accounts and money market mutual funds. (Note: You can approximate the number of years it will take to double your funds at alternative interest rates by simply dividing the yield into seventy. This is sometimes referred to as the Rule of 70.)

6. See Jeremy J. Siegel, *Stocks for the Long Run,* 3rd ed. (New York: McGraw-Hill, 2002), 342–43.

7. See Burton G. Malkiel, *A Random Walk Down Wall Street: The Time-Tested Strategy for Successful Investing* (New York: W. W. Norton & Company, 2003), 189–90. For additional evidence that a mutual fund yielding a high rate of rate of return during one period cannot be counted on to continue to do so in the future, see Mark M. Carhart, "On Persistence in Mutual Fund Performance," *The Journal of Finance* 52, no. 1 (March 1997): 57–82.

8. Even those investing in index funds should obtain some advice from experts. There are tax and legal considerations such as taking advantage of tax-deferred possibilities, establishing wills and trusts, making wise insurance choices, etc., which do require input from specialists.

9. See Liqun Liu, Andrew J. Rettenmaier, and Zijun Wang, "Social Security and Market Risk," National Center for Policy Analysis Working Paper, no. 244, July 2001.

Glossary

adjustable rate mortgage (ARMs). A home loan in which the interest rate and thus the monthly payment is tied to a short-term rate like the 1-year Treasury bill rate. Typically, the mortgage interest rate will be two or three percentage points above the related short-term rate. It will be reset at various time intervals (e.g. annually) and thus the interest rate and monthly payment will vary over the life of the loan.

Alt-A loans. Loans extended with little documentation and or verification of the borrowers' income, employment, and other indicators of their ability to repay. Because of this poor documentation, these loans are risky.

average tax rate. The percentage of one's income paid in taxes.

balanced budget. The state of government finances when current government revenue from taxes, fees, and other sources is just equal to current government expenditures.

budget deficit. The amount by which total government spending exceeds total government revenue during a specific time period, usually one year.

budget surplus. The amount by which total government spending falls below total government revenue during a time period, usually one year.

capital flight. Liquidation (that is, sale) of a country's stocks, bonds, and other capital assets and movement of the proceeds out of the country by private investors who have lost confidence in the policies of the government.

capital formation. The production of buildings, machinery, tools, and other equipment that will enhance future productivity. The term can also be applied to efforts to upgrade the knowledge and skill of workers (human capital) and thereby increase their ability to produce in the future.

capital inflow. The flow of expenditures on domestic stocks, bonds, and other assets undertaken by foreign investors.

capital market. The broad term for the various marketplaces where investments such as stocks and bonds are bought and sold.

capital outflow. The flow of expenditures by domestic investors who are buying foreign stocks, bonds, and other assets.

cartel. An organization of sellers designed to coordinate supply and price decisions so that the joint profits of the members will be maximized. A cartel will seek to create a monopoly in the market for its product.

competition. A dynamic process of rivalry among parties such as producers or input suppliers, each of whom seeks to deliver a better deal to buyers when quality, price, and product information are all considered. Competition implies open entry into the market. Potential suppliers do not have to obtain permission from the government in order to enter the market.

compound interest. Interest (the return on loaned finds) that is earned on interest that was earned during prior periods. Thus interest is earned not only on the original principal but also on the accrued interest from earlier periods.

complements. Products that enhance the value of each other and so tend to be used together. An increase in the price of one will cause a decrease in the demand for the other, and a decline in the price of one will cause an increase in the demand for the other (for example, sugar and coffee are complements, as are shoes and socks, and fast food and heartburn medication).

consumer price index (CPI). An indicator of the general level of prices. This government–issued index attempts to compare the cost of purchasing a market basket of goods bought by a typical consumer during a specific period with the cost of purchasing the same market basket during an earlier period.

Currency Board. A government entity that (1) issues a currency with a fixed designated value relative to a widely accepted currency (for example, the U.S. dollar), (2) promises to continue to redeem the issued currency at the fixed rate, and (3) maintains bonds and other liquid assets denominated in the widely accepted currency that provide 100 percent backing for all currency issued.

diversification. The strategy of investing in a number of diverse firms, industries, and instruments such as stocks, bonds, and real estate in order to minimize the risk accompanying investments.

division of labor. A method that breaks down the production of a commodity into a series of specific tasks, each performed by a different worker.

economic institutions. The legal, monetary, commercial, and regulatory rules, laws, and customs that guide how economic activity is undertaken.

economic prosperity. Persistant increases in per capita income and improvements in the standard of living.

economies of scale. Reductions in the firm's per-unit costs that occur when large plants are used to produce large volumes of output.

economizing behavior. Choosing with the goal of gaining a specific benefit at the least possible cost. A corollary of economizing behavior implies that, when choosing among items of equal cost, individuals will choose the option that yields the greatest benefit.

equilibrium. A state in which the conflicting forces of supply and demand are in balance. When a market is in equilibrium, the decisions of consumers and producers are brought into harmony and quantity demanded will equal quantity supplied at the market clearing price.

equities. Shares of stock in a company. They represent fractional ownership of the company.

equity mutual fund. A corporation that pools the funds of investors and uses them to purchase a bundle of stocks. Mutual funds make it possible for even small investors to hold a diverse bundle of stocks.

entrepreneur. A profit-seeking decision maker who assumes the risk of trying innovative approaches and products and pursuing projects in the expectation of realizing profits. A successful entrepreneur's actions will increase the value of resources.

exchange rate. The domestic price of one unit of a foreign currency. For example, if it takes $1.50 to purchase one English pound, the dollar-pound exchange rate is 1.50.

exports. Goods and services produced domestically but sold to foreign purchasers.

FICO score. A mathematically determined score measuring a borrower's likely ability to repay a loan, similar to a credit score. The FICO score takes into account a borrower's payment history, current level of indebtedness, types of credit used and length of credit history, and new credit. A person's FICO score will range between 300 and 850. A score of 700 or more indicates the borrower's credit standing is good and therefore the risk of providing them with credit would be low. FICO is an acronym for the Fair Isaac Corporation, the creators of the FICO score.

foreclosure rate. The percentage of home mortgages on which the lender has started the process of taking ownership of the property because the borrower has failed to make the monthly payments.

foreign exchange market. The marketplaces in which the currencies of different countries are bought and sold.

gross domestic product (GDP). The market value of all goods and services in their final (rather than intermediate) use that are produced within a country during a specific period. As such, it is a measure of income.

incentives. The expected payoffs from actions. They may be either positive (the action is rewarded) or negative (the action results in punishment).

incentive structure. The types of rewards offered to encourage a certain course of action, and the types of punishments to discourage alternative courses of action.

import quota. A specific limit or maximum quantity or value of a good that is permitted to be imported into a country during a given period.

imports. Goods and services produced by foreigners but purchased by domestic buyers.

income transfers. Payments made by the government to individuals and businesses that do not reflect services provided by the recipients. They are funds taxed away from some and transferred to others.

indexed equity funds. Equity mutual funds that hold stocks or other securities that precisely match the composition of a defined market basket of securities (such as the S&P 500 average). The value of the mutual fund shares will move up and down along with the index to which the fund is linked.

inflation. A continuing rise in the general level of prices of goods and services. During inflation, the purchasing power of the monetary unit, such as the dollar, declines.

investment. The purchase, construction, or development of capital resources, including both nonhuman and human capital. Investments increase the supply of capital.

investment goods. Goods and/or facilities bought or constructed for the purpose of producing future economic benefits. Examples include rental houses, factories, ships, or roads. They are also often referred to as capital goods.

"junk" bonds. High-risk bonds, usually issued by less-than-well-established firms, that pay high interest rates because of their risk.

invisible hand principle. The tendency of market prices to direct individuals pursuing their own self-interest into activities that promote the economic well-being of the society.

law of comparative advantage. A principle that reveals how individuals, firms, regions, or nations can produce a larger output and achieve mutual gains from trade. Under this principle each specializes in the production of goods that it can produce cheaply (that is, at a low opportunity cost) and exchanges these goods for others that are produced at a high opportunity cost.

law of demand. A principle that states there is an inverse relationship between the price of an item and the quantity of it buyers are willing to purchase when other things are held constant. As the price of an item increases, consumers purchase less of it. As price decreases, they buy more.

law of supply. A principle that states there is a positive relationship between the price of an item and the quantity of it producers are willing to supply when other things are held constant. As the price of an item increases, producers will supply more. As price decreases, they will supply less.

liquid asset. An asset that can easily and quickly be converted to purchasing power without loss of value.

loanable funds market. A general term used to describe the broad market that coordinates the borrowing and lending decisions of business firms and households. Commercial banks, savings and loan associations, the stock and bond markets, and insurance companies are important financial institutions in this market.

logrolling. The exchange between politicians of political support on one issue for political support on another.

loss. The amount by which sales revenue fails to cover the cost of supplying a good or service. Losses are a penalty imposed on those who use resources to produce less value than they could have otherwise produced.

mal-investment. Mal-investment is misguided (or excess) investment caused when the Fed holds interest rates artificially low, encouraging too much borrowing. The new bank credit is invested in capital projects that cost more than the value they create. At some point a correction must occur to cleanse these uneconomical investments from the system.

marginal. A term used to describe the effects of a change in the current situation. For example, the marginal cost is the cost of producing an additional unit of a product, given the producer's current facility and production rate.

marginal benefit. The change in total value or benefit derived from an action such as consumption of an additional unit of a good or service. It reflects the maximum amount that the individual considering the action would be willing to pay for it.

marginal cost. The change in total cost resulting from an action such as the production of an additional unit of output.

marginal tax rate. The percentage of an extra dollar of income that must be paid in taxes. It is the marginal tax rate that is relevant in personal decision making.

market. An abstract concept that encompasses the trading arrangements of buyers and sellers that underlie the forces of supply and demand.

market forces. The information and incentives communicated through market prices; profits and losses that motivate buyers and sellers to coordinate their decisions.

monetary policy. The deliberate control of the national money supply and, in some cases, credit conditions, by the government. This policy establishes the environment for market exchange.

money. The asset that is commonly used to pay for things; the medium of exchange most commonly used by buyers and sellers.

money interest rate. The interest rate measured in monetary units, often called the nominal interest rate. It overstates the real cost of borrowing during an inflationary period.

money supply. The supply of currency, checking account funds, and traveler's checks in a country. These items are counted as money because they are used as the means of payment for purchases.

mortgage backed securities. Securities issued for the financing of large pools of mortgages. The promised returns to the security holders are derived from the mortgage interest payments.

mortgage default rate. The percentage of home mortgages on which the borrower is 90 days or more late with the payments on the loan or the loan is in the foreclosure process. This rate is sometimes referred to as the serious delinquency rate.

national debt. The sum of the indebtedness of a government in the form of outstanding interest-earning bonds. It reflects the cumulative impact of budget deficits and surpluses.

national income. The total income earned by the citizens of a country during a specific period.

nominal return. The return on an asset in monetary terms. Unlike the real return, it makes no allowance for changes in the general level of prices (inflation).

occupational licensing. A requirement that a person obtain permission from the government in order to perform certain business activities or work in certain occupations.

open markets. Markets that suppliers can enter without obtaining permission from governmental authorities.

opportunity cost. The highest valued alternative good or activity that must be sacrificed as a result of choosing an option.

present value. The current worth of future income after it is discounted to reflect the fact that revenues received in the future are worth less now than those received (or paid) during the current period.

personal income. The total income received by domestic households and noncorporate businesses.

pork-barrel legislation. Government spending projects that benefit local areas but are paid for by taxpayers at large. The projects typically have costs that exceed benefits; the residents of the district getting the benefits want these projects because they don't have to pay much of the costs.

portfolio. The holdings of real and financial assets owned by an individual or financial institution.

price ceiling. A government-established maximum price that sellers may charge for a good or resource.

price controls. Prices that are imposed by the government. The prices may be set either above or below the level that would be established by markets.

price floor. A government-established minimum price that buyers must pay for a good or resource.

private investment. The flow of private-sector expenditures on durable assets (fixed investment), plus the addition to inventories (inventory investment) during a period. These expenditures enhance our ability to provide consumer benefits in the future.

private property rights. Property rights that are exclusively held by an owner, or a group of owners, and can be transferred to others at the owner's discretion.

productive resources. Resources such as capital equipment, structures, labor, land, and minerals that can be used to produce goods and services.

productivity. The average output produced per worker during a specific time period, usually measured as output per hour worked.

profit. Revenues that exceed the cost of production. The cost includes the opportunity cost of all resources involved in the production process, including those owned by the firm. Profit results only when the value of the good or service produced is greater than the cost of the resources required for its production.

public choice analysis. The study of decision making as it affects the formation and operation of collective organizations such as governments. In general, the principles and methodology of economics are applied to political science topics.

quota. A restriction on the quantity of a good that can be imported.

random walk theory. The theory that current stock prices already reflect all known information about the future. Therefore the future movement of stock prices will be determined by surprise occurrences, which will cause prices to change in an unpredictable or random fashion.

rational ignorance effect. Voter ignorance resulting from the fact that people perceive their individual votes as unlikely to be decisive. Therefore they are rational in having little incentive to seek the information needed to cast an informed vote.

real interest rate. The interest rate adjusted for inflation; it indicates the real cost to the borrower (and yield to the lender) in terms of goods and services.

recession. A downturn in economic activity characterized by declining real gross domestic product (GDP) and rising unemployment. As a rule of thumb, economists define a recession as two consecutive quarters in which there is a decline in real GDP.

rent seeking. Actions by individuals and interest groups designed to restructure public policy in a manner that will either directly or indirectly redistribute more income to themselves.

resource. An input used to produce economic goods. Land, labor, skills, natural resources, and capital are examples. Human history is a record of our struggle to transform available, but limited, resources into things that we would like to have (economic goods).

rule of law. The effective understanding that everyone is subject to the same laws, preventing some from enacting laws that they will not have to abide by.

saving. The portion of after-tax income that is not spent on consumption.

scarcity. Condition in which people would like to have more of a good or resource than is freely available from nature. Almost everything we value is scarce.

secondary effects. Consequences of an economic change that are not immediately identifiable but are felt only with the passage of time.

secondary mortgage market. A market in which mortgages originated by a lender are sold to another financial institution. In recent years, the major buyers in this market were Fannie Mae, Freddie Mac, and large investment banks.

shortage. A condition in which the amount of a good offered for sale by producers is less than the amount demanded by buyers because government has imposed a below equilibrium price.

shortsightedness effect. Misallocation of resources that results because public-sector action is biased (1) in favor of proposals yielding clearly defined current benefits in exchange for difficult-to-identify future costs, and (2) against proposals with clearly identified current costs but yielding less concrete and less obvious future benefits.

Smoot-Hawley Tariff. Legislation passed in June 1930 that increased tariff rates by approximately 50 percent. Other countries retaliated, and international trade fell sharply. The legislation was a major contributing factor to the Great Depression.

special-interest issue. An issue that generates substantial individual benefits to a small organized minority while imposing a small individual cost on many other voters.

Standard and Poor's (S&P) 500. A basket of five hundred stocks that are selected because they are thought to be collectively representative of the stock market as a whole. Over 70 percent of all U.S. stock value is contained in the S&P 500.

sub-prime loan. A loan made to a borrower with blemished credit or one who provides only limited documentation of income, employment history, and other indicators of creditworthiness. Federal bank regulators consider loans made to borrowers with FICO scores of less than 660 to be sub-prime. The interest rates on sub-prime loans are generally higher than for loans to prime credit customers.

subsidy. A government payment or tax credit provided to either the producers or the consumers of certain goods. The payments to producers of ethanol, which total about $1.50 per gallon, provide an example.

substitutes. Products that serve similar purposes. An increase in the price of one will cause an increase in the demand for the other, and a decline in the price of one will cause a decline in the demand for the other (for example, hamburgers and tacos, butter and margarine, Chevrolets and Fords).

surplus. A condition in which the amount of a good offered for sale by producers is greater than the amount that buyers will purchase because the government has set the price above the equilibrium.

tariffs. A tax levied on goods imported into a country.

TIPS (Treasury Inflation-Protected Securities). Inflation-indexed bonds issued by the U.S. Department of Treasury. These securities adjust both their principal and coupon interest payments upward with the rate of inflation so that their real return is not affected by the change in rate. TIPS have been issued in the United States since January 1997.

trade deficit. The difference in value between a country's imports and exports, when the imports exceed exports.

trade surplus. The difference in value between a country's imports and exports, when the exports exceed imports.

transaction costs. The time, effort, and other resources needed to search out, negotiate, and consummate an exchange of goods or services.

venture capitalist. A financial investor who specializes in making loans to entrepreneurs with promising business ideas. These ideas often have the potential for rapid growth but are usually also very risky and thus do not qualify for commercial bank loans.

List of Supplemental Units

These supplementary units are posted on the Common Sense Economics website at: http://CommonSenseEconomics.com. They have been developed as complements to this book and are freely available to all. They will be of value to instructors who want to go into more depth on any of these topics.

1. Demand, Supply, and Adjustments to Dynamic Change

2. Consumer Price Index and Measurement of Inflation

3. Gross Domestic Product (GDP): What Is It and How Is It Measured?

4. What Is the Unemployment Rate and How Is It Measured?

5. Fiscal Policy and Budget Deficits

6. Monetary Policy: How Is It Conducted and How Does It Affect the Economy?

7. The Economic Crisis of 2008: Causes and Lessons for the Future

8. Lessons from the Great Depression

9. Who Pays, Who Produces, and Why It Matters

10. Budgeting and Financial Fitness for Life

Suggested Additional Readings

de Soto, Hernando. *The Mystery of Capital*. New York: Basic Books, 2000.

Folsom, Burton. *New Deal or Raw Deal?* New York: Simon & Schuster, 2008.

Friedman, Milton, and Rose Friedman. *Free to Choose*. New York: Harcourt Brace Jovanovich, 1980.

Gwartney, James D., Richard L. Stroup, Russell S. Sobel, and David A. MacPherson. *Economics: Private and Public Choice*, 13th ed. Cincinnati: Thompson Learning/South-Western Publishing, 2011.

Gwartney, James D., and Robert Lawson. *Economic Freedom of the World, 2009 Annual Report*. Vancouver: Fraser Institute, 2009.

Haskins, Ron, and Isabel V. Sawhill. *Creating an Opportunity Society*. Washington, D.C.: Brookings Institution Press, 2009.

Hazlitt, Henry. *Economics in One Lesson*. New Rochelle, N.Y.: Arlington House, 1979.

Lee, Dwight R., and Richard B. McKenzie. *Getting Rich in America*. New York: HarperBusiness, 1999.

Malkiel, Burton. *A Random Walk Down Wall Street*. New York: W. W. Norton & Company, 2003.

McKenzie, Richard B., and Dwight Lee. *Managing Through Incentives*. New York: Oxford University Press, 1998.

National Council on Economic Education. *Learning, Earning and Investing*. New York: National Council on Economic Education, 2004.

North, Douglass C. *Institutions, Institutional Change, and Economic Performance.* Cambridge: Cambridge University Press, 1990.

Rosenberg, Nathan, and L. E. Birdzell Jr. *How the West Grew Rich.* New York: Basic Books, 1986.

Sowell, Thomas. *Basic Economics: A Common Sense Guide to the Economy,* 4th edition. New York: Basic Books, 2011.

———. *The Housing Boom and Bust,* New York: Basic Books, 2009.

Shlaes, Amity. *The Forgotten Man: A New History of the Great Depression.* New York: HarperCollins, 2008.

Stroup, Richard L. *Eco-nomics: What Everyone Should Know About Economics and the Environment.* Washington: Cato Institute, 2003.

Schug, Mark C. and William C. Wood (Eds). *Teaching Economics in Troubled Times: Theory and Practice for Secondary Social Studies.* London: Routledge Press, 2010.

Index

Entries denoted by an italic *t*, *f*, or *n* after the number indicate tables, figures, or notes respectively.

personal finance *(continued)*
  stocks in, 148, 178–82, 179*f*
  teaching children about, 148, 186–90
  used items in, 147, 166–67
  victimization and, 153
personal fulfillment, 154
personal income, 209
personal income tax
  budget constraint and, 139–40
  federal payroll taxes *v.*, 199*n*21
  subsidies *v.*, 117
politics, 105, 107
  cost *v.*, 20–21
  economics *v.*, x
  incentive structure *v.*, 29
  interest groups and, 29
  market verdicts *v.*, 126
  markets *v.*, 28–29
  opportunity cost *v.*, 26–27
  production limitation and, 25–26, 29
  secondary effects and, 36–39
  trade *v.*, 83–85
  transaction costs *v.*, 17
pollution, 12–13
pork-barrel legislation, 107–8, 108*t*, 209
portfolio, 159, 172, 175, 182–83, 185, 209
poverty, 89, 194n1
  children and, 123–24
  poverty rate, 118–19, 119*f*
  privatization *v.*, 194*n*4
  transfers *v.*, 123–24
present value, 209
president, 139–40. *See also specific presidents*
price. *See* cost
price ceiling, 209
price controls, 59–60, 209
price distortions, 105–6
price floor, 209
prices, 7, 21, 37–38, 50–52.
  See also market prices
  producers and, 18–20
  quantity per unit and, 18–20, 19*f*
private investment, 209–10
private ownership, 97
  college students and, 49

in communist China, 48–49
conservation and, 50–52
government ownership *v.*, 47–48
incentives from, 47–52
market value and, 49
price *v.* scarcity, 51–52
productivity and, 48–49
resources and, 50–52
rule of law and, 52–53
in Soviet Union, 48
stewardship and, 47–48
use of, 46–47
private property rights, 210
private-sector output, 104
privatization, 49, 132
  poverty *v.*, 194*n*4
Privatization Watch, 132
producers
  costs and, 10
  prices and, 18–20, 19*f*
production, 93
  consumption *v.*, 25, 29
  by government, 96, 97–99
  limitation of, politics and, 25–26, 29
productive assets, human capital *v.*, 30–31
productive resources, 210
productivity, 210
  favoritism *v.*, 102–3, 116–18
  government *v.*, 100
  high tax rates *v.*, 73–75
  income *v.*, 81–82
  inflation rates *v.*, 69–70
  investment for, 30–31
  present *v.* history, 30
  private ownership and, 48–49
  subsidies *v.*, 117
  transfers and, 120–21
profit, 3, 210
  costs *v.*, 21–23
  of entrepreneurs, 157
  value and, 21–23
profit-and-loss mechanism
  favoritism *v.*, 102–3
  in market allocation *v.* political process, 102–3
property, 46

About the Authors

James D. Gwartney holds the Gus A. Stavros Eminent Scholar Chair at Florida State University, where he directs the Stavros Center for the Advancement of Free Enterprise and Economic Education. He is the coauthor of *Economics: Private and Public Choice* (South-Western/Cengage Learning), a widely used principles of economics text that is now in its thirteenth edition. He is also coauthor of *Economic Freedom of the World*, an annual report that provides data on the institutions and policies of 141 countries. He served as chief economist of the Joint Economic Committee of the U.S. Congress during 1999–2000. He is a past president of the Southern Economic Association and the Association for Free Enterprise Education. His Ph.D. in economics is from the University of Washington. A member of the Mont Pelerin Society, Gwartney was invited by the Putin administration in March 2000 to make presentations and have discussions with leading Russian economists about the future of the Russian economy. In 2004 he received the Adam Smith Award of the Association of Private Enterprise Education.

Richard L. Stroup is professor emeritus of economics at Montana State University, adjunct professor of economics at North Carolina State University, and president of the Political Economy Research Institute in

Raleigh, North Carolina. His Ph.D. is from the University of Washington. From 1982 to 1984 he served as director of the Office of Policy Analysis at the U.S. Department of the Interior. Most recently Stroup has published and spoken about global warming, land use regulation, archaeology, and needed environmental policy improvements. He publishes in professional journals and popular media outlets, and his work helped to develop the approach known as free market environmentalism. He is coauthor of a leading economics principles text, *Economics: Private and Public Choice*, now in its thirteenth edition. His book *Eco-nomics: What Everyone Should Know About Economics and the Environment* (Washington: Cato Institute, 2003) was sponsored by the Property and Environment Research Center, where he is a senior fellow. He continues to research alternative institutional arrangements for dealing with climate change, regulatory takings, and other environmental risk policies.

Dwight R. Lee received his Ph.D from the University of California, San Diego, in 1972. Since that time he has had full-time tenured faculty appointments at the University of Colorado, Virginia Tech University, George Mason University, and the University of Georgia, where he was the Ramsey Professor of Economics and Private Enterprise from 1985 to 2008. He is currently the William J. O'Neil Professor of Global Markets and Freedom at Southern Methodist University in Dallas. Professor Lee's research has covered a variety of areas including the economics of the environment and natural resources, the economics of political decision making, public finance, law and economics, and labor economics. During his career Professor Lee has published over 135 articles in academic journals and over 240 articles and commentaries in magazines and newspapers; has coauthored 14 books; and has been the contributing editor of 4 others. He has lectured at universities and conferences throughout the United States as well as in Europe, Central America, South America, Asia, and Africa. He was president of the Association of Private Enterprise

Education for 1994–95 and president of the Southern Economic Association in 1997–98.

Tawni H. Ferrarini is the Sam M. Cohodas Professor and the director of the Center for Economic Education and Entrepreneurship at Northern Michigan University. She is the inaugural recipient of the National Association of Economic Educators' Abbejean Kehler Award and received the 2009 Michigan Economic Educator of the Year Award and an NMU Distinguished Faculty Award. Her work for the Council on Economic Education and reputation as a workshop leader on both the use of technology in the classroom and the integration of economics and American history helped her earn these awards. She teaches a variety of online courses regularly and employs technology tools to structure successful online courses and workshops in economic education. Dr. Ferrarini publishes in economic education, technology, and education journals on how to effectively employ technology and to successfully motivate the current generation of students. She regularly contributes to Econ4u.org and writes for newspapers on economic education, entrepreneurship, and personal finance. She earned her doctorate in economics from Washington University, where she studied under the 1993 Nobel laureate Douglass C. North.